Oops!
What To Do When
Things Go Wrong

Pat Freeland
Mike Miller

Oops! 1-2-3

Copyright© 1993 by Que® Corporation

Library of Congress Catalog No: 93-83384

ISBN: 1-56529-193-x

96 95 94 93   4 3

Interpretation of the printing code: the rightmost double-digit number is the year of the book's printing; the rightmost single-digit number, the number of the book's printing. For example, a printing code of 93-1 shows that the first printing of the book occurred in 1993.

Screen reproductions in this book were created with Collage Plus from Inner Media, Inc., Hollis, NH.

This book covers all releases of 1-2-3.

Publisher: Lloyd J. Short

Associate Publisher: Rick Ranucci

Operations Manager: Sheila Cunningham

Publishing Plan Manager: Thomas H. Bennett

Marketing Manager: Ray Robinson

Credits

Title Manager
Don Roche, Jr.

Acquisitions Editor
Chris Katsaropoulos

Production Editors
Jodi Jensen
Mike LaBonne

Editors
Lori Cates
Susan Pink
Kathy Sabotin

Technical Editor
David Rourke

Novice Reviewer
Melissa Keegan

Illustrator
John Alberti

Book Designer
Scott Cook

Production Team
Claudia Bell
Julie Brown
Jodie Cantwell
Michelle Cleary
Brook Farling
Heather Kaufman
Bob LaRoche
Jay Lesandrini
Caroline Roop
Linda Seifert
Johnna VanHoose

Composed in *ITC Garamond* and *MCPdigital*
by Que Corporation

Dedication

To Vicki, Michael, and Catherine — I love you very much.

Trademarks

All terms mentioned in this book that are known to be trademarks or service marks have been appropriately capitalized. Que Corporation cannot attest to the accuracy of this information. Use of a term in this book should not be regarded as affecting the validity of any trademark or service mark.

1-2-3 is a registered trademark of Lotus Development Corporation. Microsoft Windows is a trademark of Microsoft Corporation.

About the Authors

Pat Freeland is a former educator, now a Design Verification Engineer with Lotus Development Corporation. He has been part of the quality assurance effort for several Windows and DOS releases of 1-2-3. He is also an instructor of software, including word processing, spreadsheet, and database products. He lives on the South Shore of the Massachusetts coastline with his wife and two children and their Great Dane, Winston.

Mike Miller is the Director of Market Strategies for Prentice Hall Computer Publishing. A user of computers and computer software for more than a decade, others in the office often call on him when they have problems with their PCs. Mike is the author of over a dozen computer books, including other books in the *Oops!* series and *Real Men Use DOS* for Que.

Contents at a Glance

Contents

III A Quick Course in Problem Solving

INTRODUCTION

Some people sit down at a computer and radiate a sense of composure, competence, and complete confidence at the keyboard. Their fingers ripple over the keys, they mutter obscure phrases about what they're doing, and they seem to make no mistakes.

Other people sit at the computer with the expression of a trapped animal, looking as if they think that the next keystroke will somehow cause the end of the world.

Computer users in both categories run into problems—caused either by their own mistakes or by some quirk of the program. That's why this book exists.

Oops! 1-2-3 shows you what to do when you run into problems with 1-2-3. A worksheet program used by tens of millions of people around the world, 1-2-3—just like most software programs—can cause you problems if you're not careful. And most computer problems—including 1-2-3 problems—are caused by human error. It's very easy to press the wrong key, click on the wrong item, or type an incorrect command, whether you're working with 1-2-3 for the first time or you use it every day. In this book, you'll learn how to avoid common mistakes and correct and recover from those times when you—or 1-2-3 itself—do something wrong.

Who Should Read This Book?

Oops! 1-2-3 is for anyone who runs into a problem using any version of 1-2-3. You don't have to be a technical expert to read this book because you won't be getting into a lot of technical mumbo-jumbo. You'll learn how to cope with common 1-2-3 problems and figure out how to get things back to normal. The comments and advice in this book mix common sense with some tricks you might not know about. The goal is to get you up and running in the shortest possible time with the least possible fuss.

Why should you read this book? You should read it if you're having trouble with 1-2-3. In addition, reading this book before you experience trouble can help you avoid problems with 1-2-3 in the future. You'll be surprised at the simple steps you can take to minimize the chance that things will go wrong with your computer system.

What's in This Book?

This book has three sections. Part I, "Start Here Before Things Go Wrong," gives you valuable pointers for surviving the curves and bumps of using 1-2-3.

Part II, "Figuring Out What Went Wrong," deals with categories of problems in 1-2-3 based on the areas people most often use.

Part III, "A Quick Course in Problem Solving," gives additional pointers. This section provides an overview of the different releases of 1-2-3, the more common error messages you might encounter, "The Great 1-2-3 Troubleshooting Road Map," and the "Oops! 1-2-3 Glossary." This section should help you in tracking down and understanding your porblems.

Conventions Used in This Book

Oops! 1-2-3 uses certain conventions to help you more easily understand the text.

1-2-3 commands are preceded either by a slash (/), or if you're in Wysiwyg, a colon (:).

Italic text indicates words or phrases introduced and explained for the first time, such as *macro*.

Words and keys that you press or type are indicated in a second color, as in A1..B3.

On-screen prompts and messages (including error messages) are indicated by a special typeface and are also in a second color, as in Invalid cell or range address.

Keyboard keys are usually represented as they appear on your keyboard, such as F1 and Esc.

Key combinations are represented with the plus sign and indicate that you press and hold one key while you also press the other, as in Alt+F5.

Key combinations are represented with a comma if the one key is pressed, and then the other, as in End, Home.

Using Other Que Books

We don't intend for *Oops! 1-2-3* to be the only book you'll ever read about 1-2-3, so if you want a more comprehensive guide, you should pick up one or more additional Que 1-2-3 books. We recommend the following:

- *Using 1-2-3 Release 2.4*, Special Edition and *Using 1-2-3 Release 3.4*, Special Edition. These are comprehensive references and tutorials that tell you all you'll ever need—or want—to know about 1-2-3.

- *Easy 1-2-3*, 2nd Edition. A four-color guide to basic 1-2-3 techniques.

- *1-2-3 Release 2.4 Quick Reference* and *1-2-3 Release 3.4 Quick Reference*. Compact references that provide quick access to commands and functions in 1-2-3 Releases 2.4 and 3.4.

Good luck with 1-2-3. Don't be afraid to experiment with the keystrokes, but make your work sessions and your experiment sessions separate. Most of all, be sure to read Chapter 5, "An Ounce of Prevention: Preparing a 1-2-3 Survival Kit," so that you'll never feel the urge to "strike any key when ready" ...with a baseball bat.

Pat Freeland & Mike Miller
March 1993

Start Here Before Things Go Wrong

The 10 Most Common 1-2-3 Problems

IMPORTANT: **Please read this chapter first!**

We all know how much of a hassle it can be using 1-2-3. That's why this book begins with a list of the 10 most common 1-2-3 problems. This chapter describes the most likely causes of these problems and prescribes some easy ways to fix them. Chances are you will find your current problem on this list. So if 1-2-3 is acting mischievous, look here before you read any further.

This doesn't mean you shouldn't read the rest of this book, however. We especially recommend Chapters 2 through 5, which teach you how to prepare for and protect yourself from many common 1-2-3 problems. You should also turn to Chapter 23 for "The Great 1-2-3 Troubleshooting Road Map," which leads you through the whole gamut of 1-2-3 problems and tells you where in this book to find solutions.

The Most Common Cause

Although virtually thousands of potential 1-2-3 problems exist, the most common cause is simple: You Did Something Wrong! For example, you might have typed something wrong, accidentally pressed the wrong key, inadvertently clicked on the wrong object, or maybe you just didn't know what to do to begin with. In any case, most 1-2-3 problems are not the fault of 1-2-3 (except for its being overly complex and obtuse, of course).

So when you run into trouble and feel moved to exclaim, "Oops!" follow these simple steps to cure the problem:

1. Try the procedure again.

2. If the problem persists, make certain that you're correctly doing what you're trying to do.

3. Try the procedure one more time.

4. Check the following list for the top 10 problems people encounter when using 1-2-3.

5. Check the chapter in this book that relates to the problem you're having.

6. Strangle your computer.

If one of these steps doesn't alleviate the problem, take a look at the following top 10 list. Most 1-2-3 users can find their solutions right here; if you don't find yours in this list, read the rest of the book!

1. 1-2-3 Won't Start

The most likely cause is that you're not getting along well with DOS. To start 1-2-3, you must be in the proper directory, then type the command 123. Reading between the lines here, you can see that there are several places where you could make a mistake.

First, be sure that you're working in the proper disk drive. You might have several hard drive letters (C, D, and so on). If the 1-2-3 directory is in the D drive and you're in the C drive, you have a problem. Switch to the proper drive by typing its letter and a colon and pressing Enter.

Now, get into the proper directory. Type CD 123r23. A note here. You might have a different directory name. For example, if you have 1-2-3 in a directory called Lotus, then type CD Lotus. (DOS doesn't care whether you type lowercase or uppercase letters.)

> **Someone Stole My 1-2-3!**
>
> A student once said, with a great deal of surprise, that he checked out a computer in a store and it didn't have 1-2-3 on it! Right, you have to buy the computer and then you have to buy 1-2-3. The point is, don't assume that a program is on the computer. The steps provided here to start 1-2-3 assume that you already bought and installed 1-2-3 on your hard disk.

After you're in the proper directory, type 123. The program should start. Chapter 6 deals with this topic.

2. 1-2-3 Crashes or Freezes Up

All is not lost. If you saved your file previously—but haven't saved your most recent work—then your file still exists. Only the work you put in since your last save is lost. So when you reload this file, you'll find it to be in the same condition it was the last time you saved it— minus your subsequent work.

Fortunately, crashes and freezes happen infrequently. That doesn't mean they won't happen to you. They will. They'll happen because of some strange series of keystrokes, a cosmic ray, the alignment of the planets—or any number of unknown forces that combine to make the program simply stop running. Often, you can duplicate the keystrokes you pressed to crash the program once, and it won't crash again.

You know the program has crashed because nothing works, except your temper. Tapping all the keys, pleading with the computer, trying the Esc key, nothing works. Usually you have to reboot (re-start) the computer.

Saving your work frequently keeps this problem from being too traumatic. Check Chapter 4 for more information on this topic.

3. 1-2-3 Doesn't Look Right

It's possible that the cable from your system unit to your monitor might not be properly connected. Check your cables to make sure that both ends are properly plugged in—and that your monitor is turned on and adjusted correctly.

If that doesn't work, and assuming that everything is fine with your hardware, the next thing to keep in mind is that the new versions of 1-2-3 have two different display modes. The more familiar is text mode, the traditional look of 1-2-3. The newer look is Wysiwyg graphics mode. (*Wysiwyg* is an acronym for "What You See Is What You Get.")

In Wysiwyg mode, the letters and numbers in the cells are in a different type style, and the frame with column letters and row numbers looks different.

You can tailor the appearance of the screen by using the Wysiwyg display command. Press the colon (:) and select Display from the menu. You can change the number of rows to be displayed, the colors of the screen elements, or the size of the whole display. You can even switch from color to black-and-white display and back again.

Chapter 7 has lots of details about correcting display problems.

4. You Can't Enter or Edit Data

First of all, look in the upper right corner of the screen. There is a little box with a word in it. That box is the mode indicator and the word in it should be READY. If you made a mistake, ERROR will appear there and remain until you press Esc.

Calling up the menu, or pressing certain keys starts a different phase of 1-2-3 and temporarily makes entry or editing of data impossible. The indicator will change to show this change.

Check the indicator, if it doesn't say READY and you really want to enter data right now, press Esc until it does say READY and you're back at work.

Be sure you type a cell entry in the form acceptable to 1-2-3 or expect to run into problems. For example, typing a number followed by letters results in a beep because 1-2-3 assumes you're typing a value when you type a number first. According to 1-2-3, values have no letters in them.

Also, know the differences between labels and values. There are several important differences and ignoring them can cause data entry to be confusing.

Chapter 9 is your resource when data entry or editing becomes a problem.

5. Your Data Disappears

This problem is most often caused by the careless tap of a key that moves the cell pointer. You find yourself far away from your data and feel a terrible sense of loss. Press the Home key to return to cell A1 or the F5 (GoTo) key and the address you'd like to go to. This takes you back to your data.

Of course it may not be all that simple; you may have retrieved a file, erased the current worksheet, or deleted some cells where data was once stored. These commands are not to be taken lightly—their effects can be somewhere between troubling and devastating.

The Undo key is a great ally in the fight against lost data. So is Chapter 10.

6. Your Data Doesn't Sort Right

The big culprit here is failure to designate the proper rows and columns for the sort. If you're not careful, extra data will be included in the sort or some data will be left behind when the rest of the data is sorted.

Making the proper choice for primary and secondary sort fields helps make everything end up where you want it, and in the proper order.

Don't forget to decide whether you want ascending or descending order. Overlooking this step may sort your data in the wrong order.

In addition to sort is the mine field of data query commands that require a bit of study before you can get them to work properly.

If you need more information, check out Chapter 11.

7. Your Formulas Don't Work Right

There are lots of ways to mess up a formula. For example, using the wrong cell references, typing in the wrong arguments for the @ functions, and forgetting the proper format for the formula you're typing are just a few.

Taking data used in a formula and moving it to a new cell can cause the formula to return ERR. Copying a formula might return strange results if you used an absolute cell reference.

Most disastrous of all is a circular cell reference. Check Chapter 13 for a more complete listing of these and other problems.

8. 1-2-3 Doesn't Print Right

The most important step is to make sure that a printer has been selected before you print. Then make sure that an interface (printer port) has been selected. There'll be no printing at all without these steps.

Remember that you'll get different results depending on whether you use the Wysiwyg or the main print menu. Each of these menus contains lots of choices for changing the appearance of the final printed page.

You have a great deal of control over exactly what data is printed, where page breaks are inserted, how the printout will look, and how much material appears on each page. These topics and more are covered in Chapter 14.

9. You Can't Create a Graph

Start by highlighting the proper ranges for each element of the graph. Continue by getting into Wysiwyg graphics mode. If you're in text mode, you can create a graph but you can't see it when you add it to the worksheet.

Assuming that you performed all the steps in the main graph menu, the chances are that you added the graph incorrectly. You can type the name of a nonexistent graph and place it in a range. The name will appear in the control panel, but because there is no graph of that type or with the name you designated, no graph appears.

For help with this complicated menu, consult Chapters 18 and 19.

10. You Can't Remember How to Do Something

Buying this book was, of course, your smartest move. This, plus the documentation, should be close by when you're working in 1-2-3.

But for those times when you need a quick reminder, press F1 (the Help key) and select the topic on which you need help. Even better, start a procedure, then press F1 and you'll get *context-sensitive* help, which means you'll get a help screen on the current command or procedure.

For example, you might suddenly forget how to use the Copy command. Press the slash key, highlight the word Copy in the menu, and then press F1. Help on the Copy command appears on-screen. At the bottom of the help screen are some selections of other related topics you can highlight and read about.

Other Problems

If your specific problem isn't addressed in this chapter, don't panic. This book contains 22 additional chapters, one of which probably holds the key to your current situation. If you can isolate the general cause of your problem (printing, graphing, and so on), turn to the chapter that addresses that topic. If you can't determine even the general problem area, go directly to Chapter 23, "The Great 1-2-3 Troubleshooting Road Map," to help you identify the likely culprit. If you receive an error message, check out Chapter 22 for more detailed information.

Don't worry if some of the information presented in this chapter seems foreign to you. Just turn the page and proceed to Chapter 2, where you receive a refresher course on the 1-2-3 basics you need to get (and keep) yourself out of trouble.

1-2-3 Basics for the Technically Timid

This chapter gives you a brief overview of 1-2-3—what it is and what it does. If you're already familiar with how 1-2-3 works, feel free to skip this chapter (we won't take offense). If you're a complete novice, you'll probably want to stop here and pick up a more comprehensive Que book (such as *Using 1-2-3* or *Easy 1-2-3*) that does a more thorough job of teaching you the basics. If you just need a refresher course, however, this is the chapter for you. Turn the page and read on!

So, Just What Is 1-2-3?

1-2-3 is a spreadsheet—an electronic version of the large sheets of paper with rows and columns that accountants use. There are several versions of 1-2-3, each identified by a specific *release number*, such as Release 2.4 or Release 3.4. (For more information on the differences between versions, see Chapter 21.)

Name That Product!

Before moving on, let's establish what the name of this software really is. Many people refer to this product as *Lotus*, but that's actually the name of the company which produces the spreadsheet known as *1-2-3*. Lotus also produces many other fine software products. Calling the spreadsheet *Lotus,* instead of *1-2-3,* is a lot like saying you drive a General Motors instead of saying you drive a Corvette.

Like paper spreadsheets, 1-2-3 has rows (represented as numbers down the left side of the screen) and columns (represented as letters across the top of the spreadsheet). The point at which a column and a row intersect is called a *cell*. Each cell has a name, or more correctly an *address,* which is its column letter and row number.

So the place where column A intersects with row 1 is cell A1. Whenever you refer to a cell, be sure to put the letter first. It is always *A1*, like the steak sauce. If you refer to it backwards (1A), 1-2-3 won't know what you're talking about.

One major difference between a 1-2-3 spreadsheet and the paper ledgers used by accountants is size. A single 1-2-3 spreadsheet can contain 8,192 rows and 256 columns, lettered from A to Z, AA to AZ, BA to BZ, and so on, to IV. That amounts to over 2 million cells. Quite a spread! Compare that single 1-2-3 spreadsheet to the number of paper ledger sheets you would need to handle 2 million cells. It's pretty mind-boggling.

Other ways in which a paper ledger sheet and 1-2-3 differ are the areas you see on-screen besides the actual spreadsheet area. The area above the spreadsheet consists of three lines and is called the *control panel*. The top line of the control panel tells you what cell the cell pointer is in and the contents, if any, of that cell. The second line displays a cell entry as you type or edit it.

Naturally, there are times when you want to take actions beyond data entry. Often these actions are part of a group of commands included in the menu. To see the menu and make it active, you press the slash key (/) to access the 1-2-3 main menu and the colon key (:) to access the Wysiwyg menu. When you invoke either the main menu or the Wysiwyg menu, the second line of the control panel displays the menu choices, and the third line displays an explanation of the highlighted menu item.

In the upper right corner of the control panel is the *mode indicator*. It's important to get 1-2-3 "in the mode"—specifically, the READY mode—before it can accept data. The indicator tells you in which mode 1-2-3 is currently operating, such as EDIT, READY, ERROR, LABEL, POINT, and VALUE. Each mode tells you something about 1-2-3's current condition, so you know what you can do next or what 1-2-3 is doing. When 1-2-3 is in the EDIT mode, for instance, you can edit the contents of an individual cell. The following example points out the primary areas of a 1-2-3 spreadsheet:

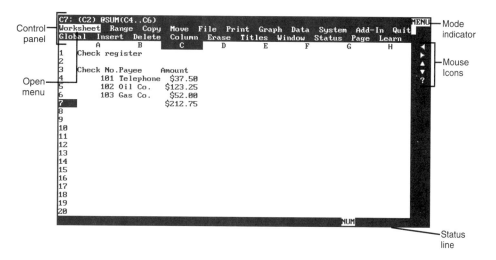

The most important difference between 1-2-3 and an accountant's paper spreadsheet is that 1-2-3 enables you to write powerful formulas to perform math calculations and otherwise process data for you. We'll look at this feature a little later in this chapter.

Menu, Please

You can access many 1-2-3 operations by using the 1-2-3 menu system. By pressing / (for the main menu) or : (for the Wysiwyg menu), you call to the control panel a list of possible actions you can take in 1-2-3. The main menu lets you tailor the program to your needs: to move, copy, and change the appearance of data, and to rearrange your data. The Wysiwyg menu allows you to change the appearance of the spreadsheet by adding new type styles, lines, colors, and other display characteristics.

You also can use your mouse to access the menus. Slide your mouse cursor to the top of the screen, and the main menu appears. If you want to switch from the main menu to the Wysiwyg menu or back again, press the right mouse button. Highlight the command you want and click the left mouse button.

Get Smart

If you are using Release 2.4, you can perform many actions by using the *SmartIcons* on the right side of the screen. Point to an icon with the mouse and click the left button to invoke the command associated with that icon. Confused about what an icon does? Highlight the icon and press the right mouse button and a short description of the icon's function appears in the control panel.

Notice the menu consists of two lines. The top line is the list of active choices. The second line does one of two things: it either shows you what menu items are available when you select a highlighted menu item in the top row, or it gives you a brief explanation of what the highlighted command does.

Simple Data Entry Made Simpler

The most elementary use of 1-2-3 is putting words and numbers into cells. This is easy enough. You use the left-, right-, up-, or down-arrow key (or your mouse) to move to the cell in which you want to place a particular piece of data; then type the data. When you want to enter numbers, type only the number and any necessary decimal places. Shortly, you'll learn how to change the appearance of numerical data.

The final step in data entry is placing the data in the cell. First, make sure the data looks the way you want it to. Use the Backspace key (the little backpointing arrow key, normally located at the top of your keyboard) to correct any typos. When the data looks correct, press the Enter key or use an arrow key to move to the next cell in which you want to place data. Either of these actions enters the data you just typed into the cell.

If you have already entered data into a cell and then notice that it's wrong, place the cell pointer in the cell containing the mistake and retype the entry—but be more careful this time. If the entry is a long one and you don't feel like typing the whole thing again,

> **I Shot an Arrow into a Cell...**
>
> You can eliminate a step by using the arrow keys to enter data instead of pressing Enter. For example, the fastest way to enter a list of 100 names in a column is to type a name, press the down-arrow key, type the next name, press the down-arrow key, and so on. If you press Enter and then the down-arrow key, you are pressing the Enter key 100 times unnecessarily...and I'm sure you have better ways to spend your time.

press F2 (the Edit key) and use the left- and right-arrow keys to move back and forth in the entry to correct it. Then press Enter. You must either press Enter to complete the editing process or press Esc to abandon the editing—those are your only choices.

Formulas Take Form

Using 1-2-3's power to its fullest involves writing formulas to manipulate the numbers you enter. A 1-2-3 formula is just like any mathematical formula—you take one or more items (normally the contents of a cell) and perform calculations. You can add, subtract, multiply, and divide items, and even apply special functions that perform specific operations.

When you're writing a formula, remember some simple rules:

- Make sure you're in the cell you want to be in

- Use cell addresses instead of plain numbers whenever possible

Why use cell addresses instead of numbers? It's easier to refer to a single cell address in formulas because when you change the contents of that cell, the other cells and formulas that use the information contained in that cell are automatically updated. Otherwise, you'd have to go to every cell and change the number manually. By using cell addresses instead of the numbers in the cells, you enable 1-2-3 to keep up with any changes you make to data. But that's not all. If you use cell addresses, you can use the Copy command to copy formulas to cells with identical functions, rather than entering the formulas again and again.

- Start formulas with a plus sign (+) that otherwise would begin with a letter

- Don't put spaces in formulas

- Avoid doing the math in your head

For example, if you want to add the contents of cells A1 and B1, you would type the following formula:

+A1+B1

Summing It All Up

Another method you can use to add the contents of cells can be a real keystroke saver—the @SUM function. *Functions* are 1-2-3 short-cuts that perform specific operations. The @SUM function, for example, lets you add the contents of multiple cells without typing the individual cell addresses with all those little + signs in between.

Getting Functional

There are many powerful and useful formulas available in 1-2-3, all of which start with the @ symbol. These include statistical, arithmetic, trigonometric, and financial formulas. You can find a complete list of these formulas and their uses in any one of Que's fine *Using 1-2-3* books.

To use the @SUM function, you type @SUM followed by the cells you want to add enclosed in parentheses. You only have to enter the first and last cells. You use two periods (..) between the first and last cell addresses to indicate that you want to include all the cells in between. For example, if you want to add the contents of cells A1 through A5, type:

@SUM(A1..A5)

Using the @SUM function is fast and easy, and it eliminates the possibility that you'll make a mistake in the middle of a long formula. The @SUM function also prevents the problem of too many keystrokes in a cell.

Pointing Out Another Way to Write a Formula

Many people prefer to use "pointing" rather than typing cell addresses. Here's how to use the pointing method. Go to the cell in which you want the answer to appear after you write your formula, and type:

@SUM(

Next, using either your mouse or your keyboard arrow keys, move the cell pointer to the bottom or top cell in the range you want to add. Now, anchor the cell pointer there by pressing the period key (.). Press the appropriate arrow key to highlight all the cells that you want to add, type a closed parenthesis, and press Enter. Voila! Your formula is entered automatically!

For those who find formulas confusing, who want to add the contents of cells, AND who have Release 2.4 and its SmartIcons, there is a simpler way. Place the cell pointer in the cell in which you want the sum to appear and click on the formula icon (the icon showing 1+2=3). All numbers are added in the cells to the left or above the cell containing the cell pointer.

Copying Made Simple

You don't want to write the same formula again and again, do you? Of course not. That's why 1-2-3 includes a Copy command. With this command, you can enter a formula once, and then copy it to other cells when you need a similar formula.

Here's Pointing at You, Kid

Here's Pointing at You, Kid

The SmartIcons that show pointing fingers are the Move and Copy icons. They enable you to designate the range to which a cell or range can be copied. Highlight the cell or range, click on the Move or Copy icon, point to the upper left corner of the range to be copied to, and click the left mouse button again. Done!

To copy a formula to another cell, follow these four steps:

1. Place the cell pointer in the cell whose formula you want to copy.

2. Use the slash key (/) to access the 1-2-3 menu, and then select Copy.

3. You'll see a prompt at the top of the screen that says Copy What? X..X. Press Enter to select the current cell.

4. Use the arrow keys to highlight the cell to which you want to copy the formula, and press Enter. You'll see that the contents of the first cell have been copied to the highlighted second cell—automatically!

Making Your Spreadsheet Look Better

After you've entered all your data and formulated all your formulas, it's time to spruce up the appearance of your spreadsheet. This is called *formatting* and can make your work look a lot more professional—which, hopefully, will result in higher self-esteem, important job promotions, and hefty pay raises.

Turning Numbers to Money

Before you start formatting numbers you must make a decision—do you want to change the appearance of all numbers or just some of the numbers? Two different command sequences are involved here.

Formatting Single Cells

Once in a while, you might want a lone number in a cell to look different from the way it does at first. For instance, a single cell may have a decimal which should look like a percent. Its value won't change, only the way it's presented. To change a value's appearance, place the cell pointer in the cell containing the value you want to change, choose /Range Format, and select the appropriate format. Finish the action by pressing Enter.

Remember, single cells and ranges can be formatted with some of the available formats by using the SmartIcons. There is one for currency, one for comma format, and one for percent.

Formatting Multiple Cells

Commands that affect a portion of the spreadsheet (as opposed to individual cells) are included under the /Range option in the menu bar. Let's assume you want to format a group of cells so that they represent money.

Move to the corner of the range of cells you want to format. Now access the menu with the / and choose Range. A new menu appears on the top command line; from this menu choose Format. When the format options are presented, choose Currency. A prompt appears asking how many decimal places you want. Choose the default for this setting, which is two, by pressing Enter.

> **Home, Home on the Range**
>
> A range is one cell or a rectangular group of cells. It cannot be oddly shaped, like a hollow frame or an L-shaped group of cells, nor can it be two separate groups of cells.

Next, use your arrow keys (or mouse) to highlight the entire range you want to format and press Enter again. All the highlighted cells are now formatted with dollar signs and two decimal places.

In Release 2.4 you can use the SmartIcons. By pressing the left mouse button with the mouse arrow in one corner of the range and dragging the mouse arrow (button still down) to the other corner, you can preselect a range. Next, click on the SmartIcon for currency ($). The range is formatted.

Clean It Up

If you entered data in particular cells and now you would like to empty them, you have two choices. The easy way to empty a single cell is to go to it and then press the Delete key. If you want to erase several cells, use /**Range Erase**. Highlight all the cells you want to erase and then press Enter.

Or, in Release 2.4, preselect the range and click on the SmartIcon that looks like a trash can.

The Wonders of Wysiwyg

Another Wonderful Acronym (AWA)

The acronym *Wysiwyg* stands for *What-you-see-is-what-you-get*. In this case, it means that you can add enhancements to the display that will appear on the printed copy. You see it on-screen and on the paper when you print. (By the way, you pronounce Wysiwyg "whizz-ee-wig.")

Your spreadsheet is done. The data is in place, formulas written, labels are realigned, numbers properly formatted. Perfection! Or is it? As they say in the kitchen gadget ads on TV, "But wait, there's more!"

There is another side of 1-2-3 that not only can make your printed work more attractive, it also makes using the program easier on the eyes. This feature is called *Wysiwyg*, and it enables you to add graphs, create desktop published-quality documents, and create dramatic on-screen demonstrations.

Hitching Up Wysiwyg

Shortly, we'll take a look at what Wysiwyg will do; but first you have to be sure it's engaged. If it is, pressing the colon key (:) will call up a menu. If it's not engaged, pressing : causes a colon to appear in the control panel. Unless you alter it or don't choose Wysiwyg when you install 1-2-3, Wysiwyg normally attaches automatically when you start the program.

Wysiwyg is known as an "add-in"; you may have to add it in to 1-2-3 while the basic (core) program is running. Otherwise, you don't even know it exists.

If you want Wysiwyg to be a permanent part of future 1-2-3 sessions, choose /Worksheet Global Default Other Addin Set and then type the first available number from the prompt at the top of the screen. Choose WYSIWYG.ADN and then No-key. (No-key means that you don't intend to keep detaching Wysiwyg. Most users keep it attached all the time and, therefore, don't need to designate a function key to reattach it.) At the question prompt, select Yes. Wysiwyg attaches before your very eyes. When it's done, select Update and Wysiwyg becomes a permanent part of your copy of 1-2-3—it will load automatically whenever you start the program.

> ### Wysiwyging Just Once
>
> If you decide to attach Wysiwyg now but you don't want it attached in future sessions, choose /Addin Attach and then WYSIWYG. Choose No-key as before. This command makes Wysiwyg available for this session only.

With Wysiwyg attached, you have a much more powerful tool at your fingertips and a more attractive display, as shown in the following example:

```
C7: {Bold} (C2) @SUM(C4..C6)                                    WYSIWYG  — Mode
Worksheet  Format  Graph  Print  Display  Special  Text  Named-Style  Quit     indicator
Column  Row  Page
```

Control panel

Open menu

SmartIcons

```
     A         B              D      E      F      G      H
 1  Check Register
 2
 3  Check No. Payee      Amount
 4       101 Telephone     $37.50
 5       102 Oil Co.      $123.25
 6       103 Gas Co.       $52.00
 8
 9
10
11
12
13
14
15
16
17
18
19
20
                                                           NUM
```

Exploring the World of Wysiwyg

Just as 1-2-3 has a main menu, Wysiwyg has one as well. You access the Wysiwyg main menu, however, with the colon (:) key. If you call up this menu by accident, press Esc to clear it.

You have a wider variety of formatting options with Wysiwyg than you do with standard 1-2-3. You can add lines, change colors, or add shading to particular cells. You can change fonts, add underline, bold, or italics to text, and when you're done, you can add a drop shadow around a range to make it stand out. You'll find most of these formatting options in the Wysiwyg menu system under the Format option.

You can also use Wysiwyg to customize the look of your 1-2-3 display. If you don't like something about the way the standard 1-2-3 screen looks, you can make changes using the Wysiwyg Display menu. For instance, you might want to change the default background color from white to some other color, or make all your text blue. If so, the Display menu is the place to make those changes.

Save That Spreadsheet!

It's a good idea to save your spreadsheet to disk periodically. (Until your spreadsheet is saved, it only exists in your computer's memory—which is erased whenever your PC is turned off!) To save a file, choose /File Save. The following prompt

```
Enter name of file to save:
```

appears at the top of the screen. Beside this prompt appears a letter (such as *C*) followed by a colon, a backslash (\), and sometimes a directory name. This line indicates the location on your disk where your spreadsheet will be saved. If your worksheet has not yet been named, an asterisk followed by .WK1 (`*.wk1`) will be displayed after the default path name for the file. Type a file name (up to 8 characters) and press Enter. 1-2-3 automatically applies the extension .WK1 to the file.

After you initially name your spreadsheet, saving your work takes only a moment. Simply choose /File Save and press Enter to accept the existing file name. 1-2-3 then prompts you with three choices: Cancel, Replace, and Backup. Cancel stops the Save operation so that you don't overwrite the previous version of the spreadsheet on your disk. Replace overwrites the older version of the spreadsheet and updates the file with your new version. Backup saves the older version of the spreadsheet to a file with the extension .BAK and saves the updated version to a file with the default .WK1 extension. In most cases you want to choose Replace, which updates the version on the disk to the current version of your work.

The Name Game

How do you name a file? Follow three simple rules. First, you can use up to eight characters in the name. Second, do NOT use spaces in the name. Third, stick to letters and numbers if you are not familiar with DOS. Because DOS accepts some punctuation marks and symbols and does not accept others, don't take any chances. Later, as you master DOS conventions and learn which symbols are allowed, you might choose to use them.

Print It for the World to See

Unless you want to carry your computer around with a long extension cord so that you can share your work with a few people at a time, you'll eventually want to print a paper copy of your spreadsheet.

Check that your printer is turned on and that you have properly positioned the paper. Start with the cell pointer in a corner of the range you want to print, for example, cell A1. Now, choose **/Print Printer**. Next, choose **Range** and highlight the area you want to print by extending the cell pointer over it. Choose **Align** to ensure that printing begins at the top of each sheet of paper. Finally, choose **Go** to begin the printing process. Before long, your efforts should yield a pristine hard copy of your spreadsheet.

If you're using Wysiwyg, you must use the Wysiwyg **:Print** command, which works very much like the main menu **/Print** command. Start with your cell pointer in a corner of the area you want to print and choose **:Print**. Be sure a printer has been selected—check the configuration box in the upper left corner of the Wysiwyg Print Settings sheet. The `Configuration` box should say `Printer:` and then display the name of your printer. If the name of your printer isn't displayed, you must choose **:Print Config** and then highlight the name of the printer you are using. Then select **Quit** to return to the next higher level of the Print menu.

Next, select **Range** and **Set**, and then highlight the range you want to print. Select **Go** to begin printing your file. Be patient—sometimes it takes a little while for all the Wysiwyg enhancements to be pulled together before printing begins.

Wrapping It Up

This has been a very brief tour of the world of 1-2-3. Note that your version of 1-2-3 may not have all the features discussed here, or may operate in a slightly different manner. If so, you may have to make some adjustments. Pick up the appropriate Que *Using 1-2-3* book for help with your version of 1-2-3.

Now turn the page and learn why bad things sometimes happen to 1-2-3 users—even you!

Why Bad Things Happen to Good 1-2-3 Users

CHAPTER THREE

You eat your greens, say your prayers, and live a good life; yet, during a session with 1-2-3, something unexpectedly goes wrong. Being a good user means you know what you're doing and you work carefully, so what could possibly go wrong? Unfortunately, lots of things. The harpies that wait to spoil an otherwise wonderful day are lurking all around your 1-2-3 program. The causes of problems are as varied as the users, and uses, of 1-2-3. It's only with extreme care that you can hold these harpies at bay.

What Are the Most Common Causes?

What *can* go wrong *does* go wrong for several reasons. First, no one knows everything there is to know about 1-2-3. Those unexplored corners of the program can be baffling, and poking around in unfamiliar commands can cause problems that are hard to fix because you don't know how you caused them in the first place.

Second, all of us occasionally make false assumptions about how things work, and those faulty assumptions can make a session with your spreadsheet extremely frustrating. Thinking a particular command does something it doesn't, writing the wrong kind of formula, getting your data types confused (labels versus values) are great examples of this frustration. Begin with false expectations, and you're bound to be disappointed.

Finally, there's always the possibility that the computer is not working the way it's supposed to. Don't be too quick to blame the program or the computer, however. Most likely, the cause of your problems is, and I hate to say this, but, well, YOU. From the moment you start installing 1-2-3 on your hard disk, you run the risk of causing any number of baffling predicaments.

The following sections describe some areas in which even the most well-intentioned users can make mistakes.

Careless Keystroking

Obviously, your work will be faulty if all the cells have misspelled labels; but careless keystroking can have much more serious consequences. Typing the wrong range for formulas, pressing the wrong keys for commands, and using the wrong cursor movement keys can cause inaccurate results, lost data, or a cell pointer placed far from where it should be. The only answer is to think before you peck at the keys, and frequently check the position of your fingers to be sure that they are poised over the correct keys.

Racing Through Your Work

When you become proficient at a particular task, you eventually do many parts of that task without thinking. Your fingers may bounce around the keyboard, thumping on keys, and leave your brain free for more important pursuits—like planning your next vacation. Then, when the brain checks in to see how things are going, it finds disaster. An example of this is the routine of saving a file.

The first time you save a file you have to name it. Thereafter, you simply choose /**File Save**, and then press Enter and choose **R**eplace. It's amazing how quickly you can press those five keys. Disaster strikes when you are saving a file for the first time and out of habit you press the same sequence of keys: /**File Save**, Enter, and then **R**eplace. Because you have not yet given this new file a name, when you press Enter, 1-2-3 uses the first name in a list of existing file names. The new data then overwrites a previously saved file whose data is gone forever.

To avoid this particular problem, you should get in the habit of using **B**ackup instead of **R**eplace as the final option in the command sequence. When you choose **R**eplace, 1-2-3 saves both the spreadsheet on-screen and in memory under the current file name, so the previous version of the file on disk is overwritten. When you use **B**ackup, 1-2-3 renames the older version already on disk with a .BAK extension, and then names the spreadsheet on-screen with the .WK1 extension. Later, if you find you

> **Speed Kills**
>
> Don't overdrive your lights. It's better to type too slowly than too fast. Racing along not only can cause silly mistakes, it can cause your computer to freeze up if you pile up too many keystrokes or commands.

made a mistake, you can retrieve the file with the .BAK extension. As soon as you retrieve it, be sure to save it using a new name so you won't overwrite it in the future. This process gives you back your original file with a new file name and the .WK1 extension.

Bad Habits

The list of potential bad habits among users is almost endless; listing all of them would be difficult. A few, however, stand out as particularly widespread.

One of the worst habits that you can develop is becoming overconfident as your skills improve. Your fingers begin to move faster than your brain works, and sometimes disaster can strike. As I discussed in the preceding section, one possible consequence is that you might, out of habit, press the wrong sequence of commands at the wrong time.

Another bad habit to watch out for is using the space bar to empty a cell. This habit is easy to pick up and has several detrimental consequences. A space consumes memory, and it can mess up your database query commands if used in the criteria range or if used in a cell in the database that should be empty. The space may make the query inaccurate.

A cell with a space can obliterate parts of labels in cells to the left when the contents of those cells are long labels that overlap the cell to the right. Long labels display as far to the right as necessary, unless there is something in the cell to the right. A space *is* something, and it will cause the long label in the cell on the left to appear to be cut off.

Get Me Outta Here!

Don't press Esc repeatedly to exit from a multi-level command if you change your mind about executing it. Many commands require you to make several menu selections before the command takes effect. Each selection takes you deeper into the command, and each one requires a separate tap on Esc to exit the command. The alternative is to press Ctrl+Break. (Break is on the Pause key.) Press that key combination just once, and you will be out of the command completely and back at READY status.

As you work on eliminating some of the bad habits just mentioned, also work on developing one particularly good habit. Always take advantage of the techniques for saving keystrokes that 1-2-3 offers. Not using these techniques will prolong your work sessions and increase your chances for making careless errors. Some users, for example, write similar formulas in adjacent cells rather than use the Copy command. Not only is this practice time-consuming and boring, it also invites key-stroking errors.

One example of wasted keystrokes is not using the arrow keys to place a cell entry in a cell. If you press Enter and then the arrow key to move the cursor after you type an entry into a cell, you'll use lots of extra keystrokes—especially on a large spreadsheet. Always be alert to ways you can save keystrokes. If nothing else, it will keep you on your toes.

Trusting Your Luck

If there is a power failure and you have not saved your work, it is lost—gone to data heaven. There is no substitute for saving your work frequently. Additionally, saving your files to a backup floppy disk is insurance against eventual hard disk failure.

> **Backups Help You Sleep Better**
>
> Knowing that no person and no hardware disaster can ruin your work is very reassuring. The only way to be sure of this is to have a copy of all your important data files on floppy disks stored in a safe place. Saving early and often is important, but so is backing up your work frequently.

Not Understanding the Meaning of Commands and Procedures

Knowing the difference between Worksheet and Range commands is crucial if you want to avoid confusion or disaster. For example, /Range Erase clears the contents of a range of cells, /Worksheet Erase clears an entire spreadsheet off the screen, and /File Erase deletes a file from the disk. Beware! Confusing these commands could turn your sunny day into a very cloudy one.

Disaster stalks the unwary who use /Worksheet Delete to clean out a few cells. This will slash a complete row or column and its data, not just a few cells.

Using **Reset** in the **Graph** or **Data** menus quickly and efficiently clears all range assignments. Again, not a command to be used inadvertently.

To avoid formula problems, be sure you understand how 1-2-3 assigns names to ranges. The range you are naming is defined by its upper left and lower right corners. If you delete either of those cells, the range name is also deleted. Formulas that previously referred to that range suddenly may return ERR. Moving those cells without moving the entire range can have strange results. Refer to Chapter 8, "What To Do When … Your Copy Won't Copy and Your Move Won't Move," and Chapter 13, "What To Do When … Your Formulas Don't Formulate," for more details about this subject.

It's also important for you to understand how to pick range names. For instance, naming a range EF92 for Expense Figures 1992 is a mistake, because EF92 is a cell address. A formula asked to sum EF92 would return the sum of that one cell, not the named range. Using macro key names such as GRAPH or CALC can cause strange things to happen in your spreadsheet if you are running macros. Placing a hyphen in a range name (NET-TAX, for example) can result in the two ranges, NET and TAX, being subtracted. If you must have a symbol in your range name, use an underscore (NET_TAX).

What's in a Name?

When you name ranges, writing formulas and navigating around your spreadsheet is much easier and more organized. Be sure that you follow these simple rules, however, when you name the ranges of your spreadsheet:

- Don't use spaces in range names

- Use underscores rather than dashes

- Make sure range names don't look like cell addresses or 1-2-3 macro key names.

Dealing with Community Property

If your computer is used by others or if your spreadsheets are accessible to other users (on a network, for instance), you can be the best 1-2-3 user in the world and still be courting disaster. Your best bet is to use a password when you save a file so that no one can retrieve it without knowing the password. To incorporate a password when you save a file, type the file name followed by a space, and then type P. This signals 1-2-3 that you want to use a password. Next, you are prompted to type the password twice; the second time is to ensure that you typed it correctly the first time. Now, when you or anyone else tries to retrieve the file, you will be prompted to type the password. If the password is typed incorrectly, a friendly message appears saying Incorrect Password.

If others must have access to your work, consider activating the protection feature by choosing /Worksheet Global Protection Enable. Then use /Range Unprotect so that others can enter or change data only in selected cells. All other cells will be inaccessible.

Cramming the RAM

There is a limited amount of random-access memory in each computer, and it *is* possible to fill it completely. Keep in mind that I'm not talking about disk space here, but memory. The programs you are running and the data you are creating can fill up your computer's RAM. Then, before you exit the program, you save the data to a disk, which clears the data out of RAM. Activating Undo, having Wysiwyg active, creating a large spreadsheet (especially one with lots of large numbers or numbers with many decimal places), and executing certain commands all can use up your RAM. The program then may refuse to do anything else, or it may flash an annoying Memory Full error message until you free up some memory. Chapter 5, "An Ounce of Prevention: Preparing a 1-2-3 Survival Kit," covers this subject more thoroughly.

Experimenting

Admit it, once in a while you try a command just to see what will happen. Most of the time this is no problem, but every so often you set up a condition in your spreadsheet that you don't know how to correct. Recently, a couple of people in a 1-2-3 class were poking around in the Worksheet menu. Suddenly, one student found she couldn't get to the upper left corner of her spreadsheet. She had tried /Worksheet Titles Both to see what would happen. Choosing the Titles command designates rows or columns to the left and above the cell pointer to remain on the screen—no matter how far from them the cell pointer moves. The problem is, you can't move the cell pointer to those rows or columns using the arrow keys (you can get there with the F5 key). Because she wasn't sure what keys she had pressed, she didn't know what to do to fix the problem (/Worksheet Titles Clear).

Another student split the screen into two sections with two separate frames. The /Worksheet Windows command was the culprit here, and /Worksheet Windows Clear corrects the problem. If no 1-2-3 expert is handy to bail you out of these situations, however, you can spend considerable time thrashing around trying to get out of your predicament. Experimentation can be a fine way to improve your skills; just be aware of the commands you choose so that you can venture back into the menu and fix the problem. If you have any doubt or question about a command, highlight the command in the menu and press F1 (Help); then read about how the command works.

A Last Word on Dealing with Bad Things

Care and thoughtful action are the best ways to avoid the bad things that can plague the most well-intentioned 1-2-3 user. Don't trust your luck—valuable data is there only as long as everything (including you) is working right. Many bad things can be corrected—that's what this book is about. Some things, however, can be for keeps—like lost data when your program freezes.

Turn the page and learn what to do when the worst happens—1-2-3 crashes and you think you've lost all your data!

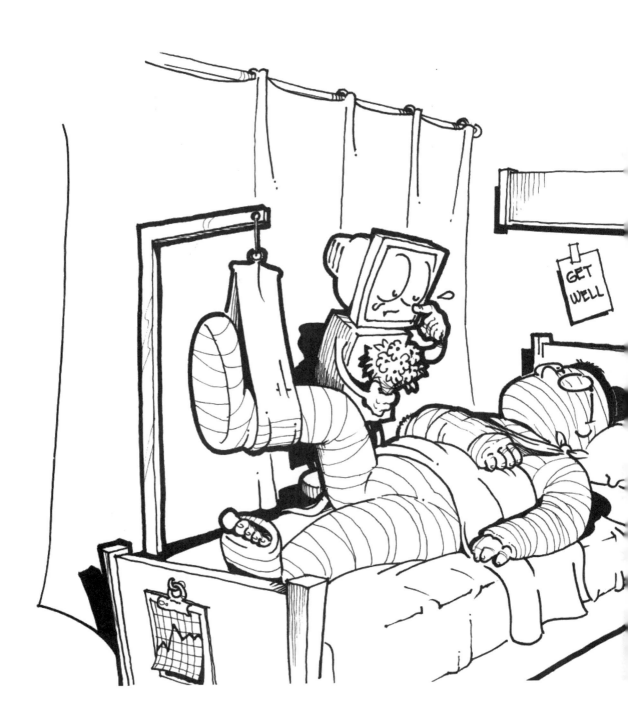

Dealing with Disaster When It Strikes

What is the worst disaster you can think of when you think about using 1-2-3? Breaking your computer? Ruining the program? Having the computer "freeze up"? Losing all your data?

Some of these can be avoided; others can be anticipated. The worst will happen—it's just a matter of time. And if it's already happened, don't assume it won't happen again.

What Is the Worst, Anyway?

I know this phrase is overused but "I have some good news and some bad news." The good news is that two of the four problems mentioned on the preceding page just won't happen. Ever. (Trust me.) There are no keystrokes you can enter that will break your computer. Yes, you can make lots of mistakes; but you can't break your computer. Also, ruining the program is extremely difficult. Odds are great that that won't happen.

The bad news is that every so often, and without warning, your computer may freeze up. It simply stops accepting keystrokes. Sometimes, it also won't let you perform certain operations.

And yes, you *can* lose all your data with a couple of careless keystrokes.

Are We Paranoid?

No, but anyone who has had one of the BIG ones happen knows how it can ruin your day. This chapter explores some of the ways you can avoid or deal with the real emergencies. Being prepared is not paranoia, it is just good sense.

The Great "Freeze"

It's usually hard to figure out what you did that caused this annoying turn of events. Even if you could remember the exact sequence of events and re-create it, there's a good chance that the computer wouldn't freeze up again. The cause is hard to figure out, but the symptoms are easy enough to spot: nothing happens on-screen, nothing works, no keystrokes are accepted. The only thing you can do when this happens is reboot (restart) the computer. Try warm booting first with the three-finger salute: Ctrl+Alt+Del. Sometimes even this won't work, and you have to cold boot— turn the computer off and back on again. Naturally, you also have to restart 1-2-3. Unfortunately, all the work you did since the last time you saved is lost and gone forever. Because you save early and often, however, this isn't a problem, right?

> ### Is It Really Frozen?
>
> When all activity stops on your computer, it most likely is time to reboot; but don't be too hasty. Try pressing Ctrl +Break (Break is on the Pause key), Esc, or Enter a few times. Then, give your computer a few minutes before you reboot. Sometimes, your program is simply taking a long time to finish a command. If it really is frozen, you don't have to rush to take action—all activity has stopped anyway.

What To Do When Your Data Is Lost

The question then is, is your data simply gone from the screen or is it completely gone from your disk? If it's gone from the screen, and if Undo is turned on, press Alt +F4 to Undo the most recent command and get your spreadsheet back. If Undo is not on, you'll have to retrieve the file and continue with your work. This assumes, of course, that you save early and often. You probably used /Worksheet Erase Yes too quickly to realize that you were using

> ### An Instant Cure
>
> Before you do anything else in 1-2-3, attach Undo. Chapter five tells you how. When attached, Undo lets you know it's on duty by placing the word UNDO in a little box at the bottom of your screen. Most mistakes you make can be immediately reversed when you press Alt +F4 (the Undo key). Keep two things in mind, both very important: Only the most recent action can be undone, and /File Save, /Print File, and /File Erase cannot be undone.

a command which clears the current spreadsheet from the screen. See Chapter 10, "What To Do When ... Your Data Does A Disappearing Act," for more information on this subject.

What Happens if You Really Do Delete a File from Your Disk

Getting an erased file back from the dead involves using the UNDELETE command in DOS 5 or using a similar command in a DOS utility, such as Norton Utilities or PC Tools.

To use the DOS UNDELETE command, first exit to DOS. At the DOS prompt, type UNDELETE, followed by a space, and then the name of the file you want to undelete. Do this as soon as you realize your mistake. Using any other save commands might make it impossible for DOS to undelete your file. Remember: the UNDELETE command is available only in DOS version 5 or later.

No sequence of 1-2-3 keystrokes can retrieve a file after you've deleted it from your disk. Your only real insurance is to keep continuously updated backup files on a separate (floppy) disk stored in a safe place. Then, if you *do* accidentally delete a file, you have an extra copy.

What To Do When You Lose the Program

There is no set of keystrokes in 1-2-3 that will delete the entire 1-2-3 program. To avoid accidentally deleting a program file using the /File Erase command (and you have to be really determined to delete a file to make this work) it's a good idea to keep your data files, the spreadsheets you create, in a separate directory from the 1-2-3 program files. Then, if you use /File Erase, files in your working directory, not the program directory, will be deleted.

In a fun-filled session with DOS, however, you might delete one or all of the program files. That's why you should always keep in a safe place a set of floppy disks containing the program. Just in case.

If it does seem that some or all of your 1-2-3 program has been deleted, you should reinstall the program. Dig out the floppy disks that contain the program, place the first disk in the floppy disk drive, and type INSTALL. Screen prompts will direct you from this point.

Where To Dump Your Data

Store your data files in a separate directory. Don't save to the directory that contains your 1-2-3 program. Keeping your data files in a directory separate from the directory where the 1-2-3 program is placed is a good idea for several reasons:

- You can locate particular files more easily.
- Your program is safer without frequent accessing, saving, deleting, and so on in its directory.
- Keeping your data files in a separate directory makes backing up, moving, and deleting them easier and safer.

Chapter 16, "What To Do When … Your Files are Funky," tells you how to use another directory to save and retrieve your files.

What To Do if You Run Out of Memory

Operations such as printing, performing a data sort, or attaching an add-in can cause your computer to run out of memory (RAM).

If memory is low, a small information flag appears at the bottom of the screen. The MEM flag designates low-memory and signifies that less than 4K of memory is available for 1-2-3. If you run out of memory completely, an error message appears in the middle of your screen. You must press Esc to clear the error message. This message means you have almost no memory remaining and nearly all actions will be rejected.

The solution to this low memory problem depends on your hardware. If your computer has expanded memory, the solution could be to kick the expanded memory into operation. To see just how much memory your computer has, choose /Worksheet Status. If you have expanded memory, the status screen tells you. In the same status screen, it also tells you whether expanded memory is set to enhanced. Look further down your screen at Cell Pointers. If it says `Conventional Memory`, engage expanded memory. Press Esc to quit out of the status screen and choose /Worksheet Global Default Other Expanded-Memory Enhanced. Be sure you choose Update from the menu you see next so that this change becomes permanent.

If you don't have expanded memory, the news is not so good. You will have to reduce memory usage. The following section explains some ways to accomplish that.

Reduce the Active Area of Your Worksheet

The active area of your worksheet is the rectangular range between the upper left and lower right cells. If possible, eliminate extra empty rows or columns in this area. Those empty cells use memory.

Press End followed by Home to find the lower right corner of your data. If 1-2-3 plunges your cell pointer way below the real data of your spreadsheet, it means you once used a cell in the row or column where the cell pointer landed, and 1-2-3 remembered that. It thinks your spreadsheet is much larger than it is. Delete all data below and to the right of the data you consider important; then save and re-retrieve that worksheet. Deleting unnecessary data empties extra rows and columns and reduces the memory used by the worksheet. Again press End and Home. You should be placed in the lower right corner of your active area. If you are still plunged way beyond the real data, you probably used the /Range Format or /Range Unprotect command on an unnecessarily large range. Using those commands on blank cells beyond where your data lies uses memory and increases the size of the worksheet when you save it. Choose /Range Format Reset or /Range Protect on all those extra cells, or, if that is too much work, see the next section for an alternative procedure.

If the Spreadsheet Is Still Too Large, Break It Up

If your spreadsheet is still too large after you've deleted what data you can, you may have to save your spreadsheet in smaller sections. Decide on ranges that you can save in separate files, and then go to the upper left corner of each range and choose /File Xtract. This command saves part of your sheet to a separate file. Next, you must choose whether to convert the cells with formulas to values during the saving process or leave them as formulas. Why this decision? Because if a formula refers to a cell that it no longer is being saved with, the formula won't work. Finally, be sure that you give a different file name to each section you save.

If You Can't Reduce the Size of the Spreadsheet, Reduce the Amount of Memory the Software Uses

If you are working on a network, try logging off and then rebooting. If you have terminate-and-stay-resident programs running (TSRs), exit them and then restart 1-2-3. If you started 1-2-3 through Windows, try exiting 1-2-3, exiting Windows, and then starting 1-2-3 from DOS. If you are using DOS 5, load any drivers in high memory in CONFIG.SYS.

Finally, Try Reducing the Amount of Memory 1-2-3 Is Using

Technonerd Talk

Every time you change something in your spreadsheet, Undo forces the RAM to remember the sheet the way it was before the change. Naturally, the RAM also has to keep the current spreadsheet in memory. Consequently, your computer's memory must have two separate spreadsheets in memory at all times when Undo is activated. Great feature, but a real memory hog.

Detach any unnecessary add-ins: Viewer, Auditor, Macro Library Manager, or even Wysiwyg if necessary. Use /Addin Detach to accomplish this.

Undo is a real memory user. You can shut that off by using /Worksheet Global Default Other Undo Disable and free up a big chunk of memory.

The Last Word on "The Worst"

As you can see, there are relatively few catastrophic things that can go wrong with 1-2-3. When they do, though, it's enough to ruin your day and send clouds of steam pouring from your head. Once the damage is done, however, it makes sense to calm down before you continue. The damage is done; racing through damage control at this point accomplishes nothing more than raising your blood pressure higher than it is already. Your best bet *always* is to be prepared for these emergencies.

10 Do's and Don'ts To Consider Before Disaster Strikes

1. *Do* plan your keystrokes carefully.

2. *Don't* race through damage control.

3. *Do* keep backup disks of your data.

4. *Don't* put off saving your work. Save early and often.

5. *Do* keep in a safe place a set of floppy disks containing the program.

6. *Don't* confuse /Worksheet Erase, /Range Erase, and /File Erase. Use them CAREFULLY.

7. *Do* be sure that your hardware is properly configured: plugs in tightly, all cables snug, expanded memory engaged (if your computer has it).

8. *Don't* be too quick to assume that the program has crashed. Wait a few minutes. Then panic.

9. *Do* keep your worksheet in a fairly small area if your computer runs out of memory easily.

10. *Don't* "strike any key when ready" with your fist. Hit a door or some other non-high-tech item.

Now, turn the page and find out how to prepare a 1-2-3 Survival Kit that can get you and your favorite spreadsheet program through the bad times.

An Ounce of Prevention: Preparing a 1-2-3 Survival Kit

Nip it in the bud. The best way to deal with problems is to avoid them. The best defense is a good offense. Care is the best insurance against disaster. An ounce of prevention is worth a pound of cure. Somehow it seems necessary to belabor the obvious in a chapter that deals with ways to avoid problems before they even start. Consider the point belabored. However trite the statements, however often they are made, they make an important point.

If your 1-2-3 sessions are to be frustration free, you must know how to provide yourself with a little disaster insurance.

Making Some Resolutions

There is no reason working with 1-2-3 shouldn't be pleasant, productive, and smooth. If you are careful and deliberate, and if you cultivate good habits, a pleasant experience is much more likely. So, before going any further, let's make several resolutions.

Follow the "First Law of Coping with Computers"

A critical resolution you should make is always to adhere to the "First Law of Coping with Computers." This "law" states simply that when you make a mistake, take your hands off the keyboard. Resist the temptation to whack away at the keyboard, pecking at random keys, and praying that one of them can correct whatever mistake you made. Are your hands off the keyboard? Now you are free to swear, stomp your feet, hit something (not the computer!), or just have a good cry. Then, collect your thoughts.

Why is this law so important? There is almost always a set of keystrokes that can correct your mistake, but often, those keys must be the very next ones you press. Pecking at other keys may make it impossible, or at least much more difficult, to correct the mistake and may introduce new problems and compound the disaster.

Don't feel that you have to rush to correct the mistake. In most cases, the damage is instantaneous; events happen in computers in billionths of a second. Trying to get to the finish line before the computer does, therefore, is hopeless. After the mistake is made, you have all the time in the world to correct it, so plan your move carefully.

Use Undo if You Can

Your second resolution should be to try to reverse your mistake by using the Undo feature that is available in the newer releases of 1-2-3. A mere press of Alt+F4 will Undo the most recent action you have taken. To use Undo, however, you first must turn it on. You can turn on (enable) Undo for the current session only, or you can make it a permanent part of every working session. To turn on Undo, choose /Worksheet Global Default Other Undo Enable.

Can You Do Undo?

Undo takes up a large amount of memory (RAM). Try enabling Undo, but watch for an error message in the middle of the screen that says Cannot enable Undo.... If you see this message, you must save and then erase from the screen the spreadsheet on which you are working before you can enable Undo. You also may have to detach other add-ins, such as Viewer or Macro Library Manager by choosing /Addin Detach.

This command sequence enables Undo for this session only. To enable it permanently, choose Update from the menu that is visible after you issue the /Worksheet Global Default Other Undo Enable command sequence. The Update command causes your selections to be a permanent part of the 1-2-3 program for all sessions. Note that when Undo is turned on, the UNDO flag appears in the status line at the bottom of your screen.

Remember, also, that only your most recent action can be undone. So, if you make a mistake, be sure the next thing you do is invoke Undo. And remember, the first law of coping with computers—take your hands off the keyboard—provides you with the opportunity to use Undo.

Don't Forget To Save

Perhaps the third resolution is the most important. Save your work early and often. When all else fails, knowing that a good, and almost up-to-date, copy of your work is safely saved on your hard disk is enormously reassuring. If you make a huge mistake, or if the computer freezes up, restart the program and retrieve the saved worksheet from disk. If you save your work frequently, you will lose very little when disaster strikes. If the last time you saved was two hours ago, you may have a lot of catching up to do. And don't forget, saving the file to a floppy disk as a backup every so often goes a long way as extra insurance.

Protect Your Work

After your formulas are in place and the main body of data is the way you want it, you can turn on the protection feature and "etch in stone" the cells that should not be changed or erased. Choose /Worksheet Global Protection Enable. This protects all cells in the worksheet; no changes can be made in any cells, and no cells can be erased. Only those cells you selectively unprotect can be changed. Use /Range Unprotect to designate cells that you might want to add to, change, or delete.

Protection is especially important if other users have access to your spreadsheets. Left to their own devices, less experienced users can make a mess out of a carefully crafted worksheet.

Password, Please

To make your work absolutely unavailable to others, save it with a password. During the process of saving a file, you are asked to type a file name. After you type the file name, press the space bar, and then press *P*. (If the file already has a name, at the prompt which says Enter name of file to save: filename.wk1, press the spacebar and then press *P*.) When a prompt appears, type your secret password, press Enter, and then type the password again. Don't forget your password, or all the king's horses and all the king's men won't be able to retrieve your file.

Restrict Input

If your work is crucial and your fellow workers are, well, clumsy, you can keep them away from valuable data by using the /Range Input command. First, however, you must unprotect the cells that another user needs to access by using the /Range Unprotect command and highlighting only the cells that require data entry. Next, enable global protection by choosing /Worksheet Global Protection Enable. Finally, execute /Range Input and again highlight the unprotected cells. Until the user presses Esc or Enter without typing a cell entry, she or he can work only in the highlighted cells.

Create a Place of Your Own

1-2-3 can be configured to save to and retrieve from a specific directory or disk drive for every session. This default directory or drive is then accessed automatically by anyone using your 1-2-3 program. To tuck your files safely away in a place separate from this default directory, you can create your own directory in DOS. Then, you can instruct 1-2-3 to use this new directory temporarily rather than using the default. With this method, it's less likely that someone will retrieve your files and damage them.

To change the current directory or drive temporarily, choose /File Directory and specify the directory or drive you want to use. When you exit 1-2-3, this instruction is forgotten and the default is restored. If you want to continue the session and restore the default directory, again execute /File Directory and specify the original drive or directory. For more information on managing files and directories, see Chapter 16, "What To Do When…Your Files Are Funky."

Hide the Goods

Another technique for protecting your work from prying eyes or from someone inadvertently deleting or changing it, is to hide the columns that contain the important data. Use

Hidden, or Is It?

Some people use the /Range Format Hidden command to hide sensitive data. This command makes the contents of highlighted cells invisible. When you place your cell pointer in the hidden cell, however, the cell contents are visible in the control panel at the top of the screen for all to see.

/Worksheet Column Hide, anchor the cell pointer, highlight all the columns you want to hide, and then press Enter. To redisplay the hidden columns, choose /Worksheet Column Display. When the hidden columns (marked with asterisks) appear in the worksheet frame, anchor the cell pointer, highlight the columns you want to redisplay, and press Enter.

Help!

Of course the best way to learn about a program is to experiment: poking into new corners, trying unfamiliar commands, and generally stretching your knowledge. As I mentioned earlier, however, if you don't know precisely what keys you pressed to cause a particular situation, you may have difficulty correcting the problem. Instead of simply trying out commands, use the 1-2-3 Help feature whenever a command is unfamiliar or you are in doubt about the correct way to use it.

Help in 1-2-3 is "context sensitive," which means that if you are in the middle of a command and you press F1 for Help, you'll get help on that particular command. Additionally, the Help information displayed will focus on the point in the command at which you are currently working.

For help on a command, access the appropriate menu and highlight the command for which you need more information. Press F1, and the screen fills with information about the highlighted command. If you want additional help, choose from among the other topics listed at the bottom of the Help screen. When you are finished with Help and ready to go back to work, press Esc.

The 1-2-3 Survival Kit

A little care and planning can go a long way in helping you keep disaster at bay. The following paragraphs recommend the essential ingredients contained in any *true* 1-2-3 Survival Kit.

Your Original 1-2-3 Disks

The first thing in your 1-2-3 Survival Kit are the original disks you received when you bought the program. They should be stored in a safe place in case the program you installed on your hard disk becomes unusable for any reason.

Copies of Your 1-2-3 Disks

Use the DOS COPY command or the DOS DISKCOPY command to make duplicates of each of the original 1-2-3 disks; then, store these backup copies separate from the original disks. This procedure gives you extra insurance in case the original disks and the program installed on your hard disk both are ruined.

Backups of Your 1-2-3 Data Files

Use the DOS COPY or the DOS BACKUP command to place copies on a floppy disk of the files you created in 1-2-3. Do it frequently. You never know when something might happen to your hard disk and cause you to lose all the files on it. The COPY command is fine if all files fit easily on a single disk. The BACKUP command is more efficient if you have lots of files and they will fill more than one disk.

If something does happen to the data files on your hard disk, simply copy your backed up data files from the floppy back to the hard disk. If you use the BACKUP command, you will have to use the DOS RESTORE command to retrieve your files from the floppy disk.

A Last Word on Precautions

For those determined to risk disaster through carelessness and haste, you're on your own. But for those who prefer a serene and successful session with 1-2-3, get in the habit of using the techniques listed in this chapter. Remember, careful and deliberate work is the most important step you can take to avoid disasters. Trying to work too quickly and not saving your work frequently are your worst enemies.

This concludes Part I, the "safety first" section of this book. Turn to Part II, "Figuring Out What Went Wrong," to find solutions to specific problems—and good luck!

Figuring Out What Went Wrong

PART TWO

What To Do When...

1-2-3 Won't Start

You won't get very far creating a worksheet if you can't get into the program. After you install and learn the proper procedure for starting 1-2-3, getting the program running is a snap... most of the time.

Sometimes the "harpies" that lurk behind your computer and make bad things happen for no reason prevent 1-2-3 from starting. This is rare. Either it won't ever start, or there really shouldn't be a problem if you execute the DOS commands correctly. The purpose of this chapter is to help you deal with two situations: You've never been able to start 1-2-3, or suddenly, it's become a problem to start.

Getting 1-2-3 Up and Running

After you install the software on your computer (assuming that you or whoever installed the software followed the correct installation procedure), you are ready to use 1-2-3. (Refer to the 1-2-3 program documentation if you need information about installing the program.)

Installing?

The purpose of the 1-2-3 Install program is to configure 1-2-3 to run with your particular hardware. It also transfers the proper working files from the floppy disks to your hard disk. In the process, Install creates a directory on your hard disk into which those files are transferred. When Install is done, you should store the floppy disks in a safe place in case something goes wrong with your computer, your hard disk, or the program.

To start the program, you have to type two DOS commands at the DOS prompt. The first command you type moves you to the directory in which the 1-2-3 program is stored. The following list shows the directory names for various versions of 1-2-3. Except for older versions of 1-2-3, the directory name used by Lotus begins with *123*, followed by an *R* for release, and the release number (without the period). The DOS command to move to a directory is CD; the entire command you type is shown in the first column of the following list:

Command You Type	*Version of 1-2-3*
CD\123	Releases 2.2 and earlier
CD\123R23	Release 2.3
CD\123R24	Release 2.4
CD\123R3	Release 3.0
CD\123R31	Releases 3.1 and 3.1+
CD\123R34	Release 3.4

The command you just typed (from the preceding table) doesn't start 1-2-3. It isn't supposed to. It just makes the computer look in the proper directory. When that is done, just type 123 (don't include hyphens) and press Enter. 1-2-3 should start.

What To Do When You Can't Start 1-2-3

Most of the time, 1-2-3 won't start because *you* made a mistake. Blaming the program or your computer should be a last option. Read on to examine the most common problems you might encounter.

Getting the Directory Right

If you told the 1-2-3 Install program to use a different directory name, you have to substitute that directory name in the command to start 1-2-3. Also, if someone else installed your copy of 1-2-3 and you don't know which version you have, try the commands in the preceding table until one works. (Better yet, contact the person who installed your program.) You'll know the command worked if you don't receive an error message such as Invalid directory.

Problem 1:

You type 123, but nothing happens

The first thing to do is type exactly the same thing again. Type 123 and press Enter. It may start this time. If the system hangs (locks up), start your computer again by pressing the Ctrl+Alt+Del key combination; then issue the same two commands to start 1-2-3. This may well be one of those times when for no apparent reason the program won't start, but it will start the next time you try.

If this still doesn't get you going, you probably forgot to type 123 in the proper

---

Driving You Crazy

Sometimes people divide larger hard disk drives into several partitions. Each partition has a separate letter, such as C:, D:, and so on. If your hard disk is set up like that, typing 123 in the wrong drive has no effect. Be sure you type the letter and a colon for the disk drive where the 1-2-3 program is located before you type any other commands. For instance, if the program directory is on the D: drive, type D: and press Enter.

---

directory. Remember that if you are in another directory and type 123 and press Enter, it is as if your computer never heard of 1-2-3. In this situation, you get a Bad command or filename error message. Type the CD command followed by the appropriate directory name for the version of 1-2-3 you are using (see the table earlier in this chapter). Then type 123 and press Enter. Your computer responds as if to say, "123! Why didn't you say so in the first place?" The program starts without a problem.

10 Do's and Don'ts To Be Sure 1-2-3 Starts

1. *Do* install 1-2-3 according to the on-screen instructions.

2. *Don't* type 123 until you are in the proper directory.

3. *Do* be sure you are on the right disk drive (normally drive C) before you change to the proper directory.

4. *Don't* use the DOS DELETE command while you are in the program directory. If you must, use it carefully.

5. *Do* type CD followed by a \ (backslash) and the name of the directory to get to the proper directory.

6. *Don't* be too quick to blame the hardware or software if 1-2-3 won't start; be sure you typed the correct commands.

7. *Do* reboot the computer and try again if at first you don't succeed and the computer freezes up.

8. *Don't* include spaces or hyphens—just type 123 and press Enter.

9. *Do* keep the original program floppy disks in a safe place.

10. *Don't* type one two three. Use the numerals.

Problem 2:

You quit another program and type 123, but nothing happens

Be sure you really exited the other program you were in. In many software packages, it's possible to issue a command that suspends the program temporarily so that you can use DOS commands. This is often called "shelling out" to DOS. The screen looks as though you're really in DOS, so typing 123 seems like the right thing to do. Remember, however, that the program you left to access the DOS command line is still running. If you type 123 at this point, you may not have enough memory (RAM) to run it, and you'll get an error message that says something like, 1-2-3 cannot start because there is not enough memory available. First, you have to get back to your original program, close it, and then start 1-2-3. To get back into a suspended program from the DOS command line, type EXIT and press Enter. (By the way, DOS doesn't care whether you type in lower- or uppercase letters.)

You use the same technique to reenter 1-2-3 if you exit it temporarily by pressing /System. This command suspends 1-2-3 so that you can issue DOS commands. Do not type 123 at this point, or once again you will get the error message:

1-2-3 cannot start because there is not enough memory available

This message appears because your computer's memory is being used for the session of 1-2-3 you still have open. Remember, you have only *temporarily* suspended 1-2-3, and the program is still running in RAM. Type EXIT and press Enter, and you will get back into your worksheet.

Problem 3:

You quit another program, you are in the proper directory, and you type 123, but still nothing happens

It's possible that the entire program somehow got deleted. It is also possible that the one file that starts the program is missing. That file is 123.EXE. Without that file, you can type 123 forever and nothing will happen. Check to be sure that this file and the entire program are still in the directory. If 123.EXE isn't there, you need to reinstall 1-2-3 from the program disks in your 1-2-3 Survival Kit (described in Chapter 5).

Problem 4:
You type 123 and the program starts, but then it stops working

Getting Right To Work

Typing 123 starts the program, but you can also get the program to retrieve a file as soon as it starts. To do this, type 123 -w followed by the drive path and file name of the worksheet on which you want to work. (If the file you want to retrieve is stored in the default directory— the directory 1-2-3 normally uses to save and retrieve files—you don't have to include the drive and directory name.) Let's say you have a file called BUDGET.WK1 in a directory called DATA on the C: drive. To start 1-2-3 and automatically retrieve the BUDGET.WK1 worksheet, type the following:

    123 -wC:\DATA\BUDGET

This is similar to the situation in Problem 3. It's likely that part of the program has been deleted. Remember the recommendation that you keep the floppy program disks in a safe place? It's time to go to that safe place, get the disks, and reinstall the program.

Another problem that can cause 1-2-3 to start and then stop is low memory. Check Chapter 4, "Dealing with Disaster When It Strikes," for advice about handling this problem.

Problem 5:
You type both the CD command and the 123 command, but the error message Bad command or filename appears

This seems to happen often to inexperienced users. Remember you must press Enter after each DOS command. People sometimes type both commands (such as CD\123R24123) before pressing Enter. You must first type the appropriate CD command and press Enter to get to the proper directory. Then, you type 123 and press Enter again. You can't pile up DOS commands and try to enter them all at once.

A Last Word on Starting 1-2-3

DOS performs the steps you take to get 1-2-3 running. Be sure you understand the proper commands and type them exactly right. Upper- and lowercase letters don't matter, but just about everything else does. Be sure you use spaces only where they are needed, and press Enter when you finish each command.

If you have a DOS expert around, or if you are comfortable with DOS, consider adding the 1-2-3 directory to the path in AUTOEXEC.BAT. Alternatively, you can write a batch file to start 1-2-3 from the root directory. Either of these procedures enables you to start 1-2-3 from any directory without having to use the CD command.

What To Do When...

Your Display Looks Funny

Nobody wants to get cross-eyed looking at the screen, and nobody wants to put up with pesky problems involving the appearance of a worksheet. There are lots of ways to improve the appearance of the display, and there are a few things to watch out for when you change the display.

Making It Easy on the Eye

Almost every command you use in 1-2-3 has some effect on how things look on-screen. Widening columns, formatting numbers, and realigning labels are among the many commands that affect the display. Because so many commands affect the way the screen looks, it might be possible for much of the information in the other chapters to be included in this one. To keep that from happening, this chapter is limited to problems with the display that make it hard to see your work and cause things to be on the screen that you'd rather not see. The chapter also focuses on ways to change the appearance of the screen to make the entire display more pleasing.

When you start 1-2-3 for the first time, you're presented with the default display. You can do many things to change the appearance of the screen. The main menu and the Wysiwyg menu both have selections that make viewing your data much easier.

The main menu offers ways to get large worksheets under control using titles, hidden columns, or windows. The Wysiwyg :Display menu enables you to increase the size of everything on the screen by changing the zoom factor. You can change the colors of most parts of the screen by using :Display Colors. You can change the shape of the cell pointer. You can also add a grid that gives each cell an outline. You can change even the frame (the upside-down *L* that displays row numbers and column letters) or remove it completely in the :Display Options part of the menu.

In the main menu, the Worksheet commands affect the entire worksheet, and the Range commands affect a portion of the worksheet. In the Wysiwyg menu, the Display commands can affect the entire screen, whereas the Format commands affect only a portion of the worksheet. Display changes remain even after a worksheet is erased from the screen. Format changes are saved with a given worksheet and disappear when it is erased.

10 Do's and Don'ts for Changing the 1-2-3 Display

1. *Do* accept the display defaults in the installation unless there is a good reason to change them.

2. *Don't* use Worksheet and Display commands to change ranges or individual cells. Use Range and Format commands for that purpose.

3. *Do* use Worksheet and Display commands to change the entire screen.

4. *Don't* forget to use /Worksheet Global Default Update and :Display Default Update to make any changes permanent.

5. *Do* have Undo enabled to correct any mistakes you make.

6. *Don't* assume the display will look like the printout when you're using colors in the worksheet, unless you have a color printer. Switch to **Display Mode B&W** before printing to be sure the printout will look presentable.

7. *Do* use **:Print Preview** also to see how the printout will look after making display changes.

8. *Don't* use **:Worksheet Row Set-Height** unless there is a good reason. Changing fonts does that for you.

9. *Do* be careful when you make selections in **:Display Options Adapter**. The screen might go blank.

10. *Don't* use too many fonts or Wysiwyg changes in your work. If you do, it may look like a ransom note or a circus poster.

What Can Go Wrong with Your Display

As you enter data and move among the various menus to tailor your display to suit your tastes, things you don't expect may happen on-screen. The following sections help you deal with some of those frustrations.

Problem 1:
When you look at distant parts of a large worksheet, the row or column titles disappear

Many worksheets are so large that they sprawl off the screen. As you scroll (move the cell pointer) away from the upper left corner of your data, it is impossible to see the titles for the rows and columns that you typed at the left or at the top. This can be very confusing.

Use /Worksheet Titles to keep certain rows or columns always visible on the screen. You use the Horizontal option to keep designated rows on the screen, the Vertical option to keep specific columns, or Both to keep specific rows and columns on the screen. Remember that when you start the command, the rows above the cell pointer and columns to the left of the cell pointer become titles. Be sure to start the command with the cell pointer in the proper cell.

Problem 2:
You used the /Worksheet Titles command and now you can't get to a cell in the Titles area

Actually, you can. Just don't use the arrow keys—they won't move you into the rows or columns designated as titles. Instead, use the F5 (GoTo) key. Name the cell you want to go to, even if it is in the titles area, and press Enter. The display might be a bit odd (you might see the same area displayed twice), but at least you're where you want to be. If that doesn't satisfy you, you'll have to get rid of the titles using /Worksheet Titles Clear.

Problem 3:

Two columns in a large worksheet are so far apart that you can't compare their information

Trying to follow data across a long row causes your eyes to wander from row to row. When long rows are a problem, hide the unnecessary columns separating the important data. Go to one of the columns you want hidden from view and choose /Worksheet Column Hide. The next step is to anchor the highlighter in this column and highlight all the other ones you don't want to see and press Enter. This command does not delete columns; they are only hidden. To redisplay data, choose /Worksheet Column Display, then highlight all the columns that have an asterisk in the frame. After you press Enter, only some columns might be visible on the screen; never fear, you can bring the others into view with the arrow keys.

Problem 4:

You want to see distant parts in a large worksheet, and hiding columns is not the answer

Here is the solution. Split your screen into two separate, smaller worksheets, each of which can look at different parts of a large worksheet. The two separate views of the same worksheet are called *windows*. They can be vertical or horizontal. In either case, the screen is split in the row or column where the cell pointer is, so position it first. Then choose /Worksheet Window Vertical or /Worksheet Window Horizontal. You can jump the cell pointer from one window to the other using the F6 (Window) key.

When you want to heal the rift you've introduced into your screen, use /Worksheet Window Clear.

Problem 5:

You created a window, but the second window moves as the first one does

Sometimes that's great; if you're looking at data in one vertical window and moving down row by row, it is nice when data in the other window follows along. At other times, you might be looking at two unrelated sections of the work and not want one window moving just because the other one does.

When you want one window to sit still, execute the /Worksheet Window Unsync command. This allows movement within one window without the other one following along. To cause both windows to move in sync, care to guess the command? It's /Worksheet Window Sync.

Problem 6:

The labels and values you typed don't line up properly

Unless you specify differently, labels are aligned at the left side of cells, and values are aligned at the right side. You can change label alignment, but you can't change value alignment.

To change the alignment of every label you type from now on, choose /Worksheet Global Label-Prefix and pick the place where you want the labels to be. You can change labels you've already typed in ranges or individual cells using /Range Label Left (or **Right** or **Center**).

Problem 7:

Your formulas return zeros, but you don't want zeros all over the place

This happens, for example, when you write a formula in a row where there is some data, then copy it to rows where data will be but isn't yet. All the formulas in the empty rows show zero, and that looks strange.

Using the /Worksheet Global Zero commands, you can choose to stop the display of the zeros, to show the zeros, or to put a given label where the zeros would appear. Why a label? One use for this feature might be in a worksheet in which you would like to have N/A (not applicable) appear in cells where there would otherwise be zeros. When the formula returns a value other than zero, it actually displays the number.

Watch this command, though, because at first glance it appears backward. After selecting /Worksheet Global Zero, the choice is **No, Yes,** or **Label. No** displays the zeros, and **Yes** does not. The reason is that you're saying yes or no to *zero suppression*, not to the display of zeros.

Problem 8:
Negative numbers are displayed with parentheses, but you prefer a minus sign

If you format the negative values with the comma or the currency format, they are displayed with parentheses. If you prefer minus signs to parentheses with these formats, you have to execute /Worksheet Global Default Other International Negative Sign. Remember that these commands affect only values with the comma or currency formats.

> **Color Me Negative**
>
> Using the Wysiwyg menu, you can change the color of negative numbers. Choosing :Format Color Negative allows you to display negative numbers in black or red. If you use the :Display Colors Neg menu, you can choose from eight colors.

A Rainbow of Colors

You can replace the eight colors offered in the Wysiwyg menus by using **:Display Colors Replace**. By highlighting the color name and pressing Enter, you can select a hue from the palette displayed. Use **:Display Default Update** to make the change permanent.

Problem 9:

You aren't satisfied with the eight fonts from which you can choose (Wysiwyg)

Enter the **:Format Font** menu and choose **:Replace**. You can replace any of the original eight fonts with a different font and size. By choosing Other, you can expand your selection beyond the basic four fonts.

Problem 10:

Tops of letters are chopped off after you format a cell with a different font (Wysiwyg)

This is caused by using the mouse or the **:Worksheet Row Set-Height** command to set the height of a row manually. It is not normally necessary to set row height manually, because the row height is automatically adjusted for the largest font in the row. You have to set the row height manually, however, when you use formatting sequences. See the sidebar titled, "Off with His Head," later in this chapter for more on that subject.

To correct the decapitated letter problem, choose **:Worksheet Row Auto**. This removes the height setting from all highlighted rows. Now when you change fonts, the row height adjusts automatically.

Problem 11:

All characters on a label you typed have the same appearance; you want a word in the label to appear in boldface (Wysiwyg)

You use formatting sequences to make items within a label different from the rest of the label. They work only in Wysiwyg graphics display mode. For example, you might type in a cell the label This text is boldface and want to boldface only the word boldface. To make this happen, start the cell entry as always, but before you type the word boldface, press Ctrl+A, and then the formatting sequence for boldfacing, which is b.

To turn off the formatting sequences you used, type Ctrl+N. To turn off just one sequence, use Ctrl+E. Suppose you pressed Ctrl+A followed by b for bold, and then again pressed Ctrl+A and i for italics. The next word would be italicized and boldfaced. After you type the word, you might want to turn off only italics. To do that, type Ctrl+E and i. That turns off italics but leaves boldface on.

The following table is a list of the formatting sequences. Note that these *are* case-sensitive: Pay attention to lowercase and uppercase letters.

Formatting sequence	Description
b	Boldface
i	Italics
f	Flashing
o	Outline
x	Flipped on label's x-axis
y	Flipped on label's y-axis
d	Subscript
u	Superscript
1_	Single underline
2_	Double underline
3_	Wide underline
4_	Box around characters
5_	Strikethrough characters
1c	Default color

continues

Formatting sequence	Description
2c	Red
3c	Green
4c	Dark blue
5c	Cyan
6c	Yellow
7c	Magenta
8c	Reverse colors (background and text)
1F	Font 1
2F	Font 2
3F	Font 3
4F	Font 4
5F	Font 5
6F	Font 6
7F	Font 7
8F	Font 8

Off with His Head

Changing to a larger font using the formatting sequences causes the tops of the larger letters to be chopped off. In this case, you need to use :Worksheet Row Set-Height to make the row higher. The rule of thumb is to make the row two points higher than the height of the letters in the row.

You can use these formatting sequences also in graph titles and legends, headers, and footers, and in the Text Edit mode. Watch out, though, if you switch out of Wysiwyg graphics display mode. The formatting sequences show up on the screen where everyone can see them in text mode.

Problem 12:

You want long labels to be centered on a cell, but they spill out of cells to the right (Wysiwyg)

When you want a long label in Wysiwyg graphics display mode to spill out of a cell to the left or be centered on a cell, use a double label prefix to accomplish this. See Chapter 8, "What To Do When ... Your Copy Won't Copy and Your Move Won't Move," for more details about this option.

An alternative is to use the :Text menu. Use :Text Align Left (or Center or Right). Then highlight the horizontal range in which you want the label to be aligned. The label slides to the right so that it is properly aligned in all the cells you highlighted.

> ### Square Away the Paragraph
>
> Use :Text Align Even on an entire paragraph in Wysiwyg to make both the left and right sides straight. Highlight horizontally and vertically to indicate the space you want the newly aligned paragraph to fill.

Problem 13:

Your display is color but your printout is black and white. You don't know how the printout will look. (Wysiwyg)

Choose :Display Mode B&W. The screen now gives a much more accurate picture of how the black-and-white printout will look. Colors and shading can sometimes make a printout hard to read, so it's a good idea to check in this mode before you print. While you're in black-and-white display mode, it's a good idea to preview your print range. Use :Print Preview.

Problem 14:

You made a bunch of display changes, but the next time you entered 1-2-3, the old settings were back (Wysiwyg)

For the changes you make in the :Display menu to be permanent, you have to select :Display Default Update. This makes any changes you've made in the :Display menu a permanent part of the 1-2-3 Wysiwyg program for every session.

Problem 15:

The blinking hardware cursor drives you crazy (Wysiwyg)

Choose :Display Options Adapter Blink No to stop the dash in the cell pointer from winking. There, is that better?

A Last Word about Your Display

Keep in mind that you have tremendous flexibility in the way you display your work, especially in Wysiwyg. Most users accept the defaults, but there is nothing magic about having a solid cyan-colored cell pointer. You're the boss. Change it to suit yourself.

Your Copy Won't Copy and Your Move Won't Move

CHAPTER EIGHT

With the Copy command, you can write complicated formulas and copy them to wherever they're needed. Or you can enter a long list of data and copy it to other locations so that it can be used in several places, thus saving the time and drudgery of typing the same data into other areas where you might need it. With the Move command, you can remove data from the original range and place it in a new range.

Because there are several steps to copying and moving data, you run the risk of making mistakes more easily or becoming confused over what data has been copied and what data has been moved. Mastering the Copy command makes these possibilities a lot less likely.

Mastering Copy and Move

For either the Copy or Move command, you must do each step in the command carefully and in order. This caution might seem obvious, but highlighting the wrong range at the wrong time is the single biggest source of copy and move problems.

Doing the Copy Thing

To get the results you want with either Copy or Move, think of each as requiring four distinct steps:

1. Go to a corner of the range you want to copy.

   Generally, the upper left corner is where people prefer to start.

2. Call up the commands and select either Copy or Move.

   Now the ticklish part begins.

3. Answer the Copy What? prompt by designating the cell or range you want to copy.

4. Answer the To where? prompt by designating the destination range for the data being copied.

   In the last two steps you can type in the cell address (A1), a range address (A1..B5), a range name, or actually highlight the range with the cursor-movement keys.

The main problem you'll experience with this exercise is highlighting too much range at the Copy what? prompt. Highlight only the cells you want to copy.

If you're copying a range, you don't have to highlight the entire range you're copying to. Put the cell pointer in the upper left corner, or type in the cell address of the upper left corner of the destination range and press Enter. All the data you're copying will arrive in the new range.

Where Copy Is Different from Move

This section discusses several differences between Copy and Move. Keep the most obvious difference in mind before you start using either command.

Copy puts a duplicate of the data you highlight in another part of your worksheet. When the command is done, you'll have two copies of the same data.

Move removes completely and permanently the data from the original range and places it in a new range.

Another major difference between Copy and Move involves formulas. After the Copy command is done, the results of formulas are different in the new cells. After the Move command is done, however, the results of formulas don't change. Move and Copy are supposed to work this way so don't be surprised.

When you copy a formula, the relative cell references are adjusted. For example, if a formula in A3 adds cells A1 and A2 and you copy that formula to B3, it will add B1 and B2. The formula's relative cell references are the two cells above it. No matter where the formula is copied to, it will add the two cells directly above it.

Not so with Move. When you move a formula, it continues to refer to the same cells it referred to before. For example, if a formula in A3 adds A1 and A2, it will continue to add A1 and A2 after being moved to B3.

10 Do's and Don'ts When Using Copy and Move

1. *Do* be in the cell you want to copy or move.

2. *Don't* highlight extra empty cells when executing Copy or Move.

3. *Do* keep the `Copy What?` and `To Where?` steps separate.

4. *Don't* expect cell references in formulas to change when you move the formula.

5. *Do* expect cell references in formulas to change when you copy formulas.

6. *Don't* copy formulas too close to worksheet boundaries.

7. *Do* check the `To` range before copying or moving to be sure you don't overwrite data.

8. *Don't* move the upper left or lower right corner of a named range without moving the rest of the named range with it.

9. *Do* have Undo enabled if at all possible.

10. *Don't* move a cell to the upper left or lower right corner of a named range.

What To Do When Your Copy or Move Doesn't Work

The following paragraphs refer to the Copy command; but, unless otherwise mentioned specifically, they refer also to the Move command. Here are some things to watch out for.

Problem 1:
You copy data to the wrong place

The best way to correct this problem is to perform Undo. Alt+F4 will undo the most recent command you performed. As always, to avoid making mistakes, take the time to plan your moves carefully. If you make a mistake, then take another action before pressing Alt+F4, Undo will reverse those most recent actions rather than the ones you really want to undo. See Chapter 4, "Dealing with Disaster When It Strikes," for instructions about enabling Undo.

If Undo is not enabled, you'll have to erase the data you copied to the new range. Data that has been overwritten is gone and will have to be reentered.

Problem 2:
You have trouble using the GoTo key during the Copy or Move command

The F5 (GoTo) key is disabled during these commands. You've probably noticed that when you have to copy data a long way, it's time-consuming to move the cell pointer to the TO range before you press Enter. In that case, you should type in the address of the TO range rather than going to it during the Copy command. Yes, this

---

Look Where You're Headed

During the Copy command, you're prompted to enter the range you're copying to. You can either type the range you want to copy to, or you can move the cell pointer to that range and highlight it. Going to the range is better because you can see whether you'll be overwriting data.

---

contradicts the advice we just gave you (check the TO range before finishing the Copy command to ensure that you won't replace valuable data with the Copy command). If it's a pain to go to the TO range during the Copy command, then go there before you start the command, check to ensure that it's empty, and then execute the command.

Problem 3:
After the Move command, some formulas return ERR

This action applies only to the Move command.

If you move data into one of the cells the formula refers to, you'll see ERR. You'll have to Undo the move or reenter the data, and then edit the formula so it refers to the proper cells.

The formula may have referred to a named cell or range. Be careful about moving data into named ranges. If you move to the upper left or lower right corner of a named range, or if you move to a named cell, the name is lost and the formula which refers to the range with that name returns ERR.

Move clears out the original cell and deposits the data in a new cell. This action turns your formula to ERR. It will make a mess out of your formulas. When it does, you either must use Undo immediately or reenter data and formulas as they were before the move. You'll also have to rename any ranges if you moved to one of the corners of that range. Use /Range Name Create, type the original name of the range, and highlight the proper cells.

Remember that when data must go into cells referred to by a formula, use Copy (rather than Move), and then delete the original cell. The formulas will work fine after this. Notice that Copy can also result in a formula cell showing ERR. For example, assume that A3 contains formula +A1/A2. If you copy A3 to B3 and B2 is blank (or nonvalue), you have a case of division by 0 (B1/B2) because B2 has nothing in it. Therefore, the copied cell will display ERR.

Problem 4:

After a Move command, the results of a formula change

It's likely that the formula referred to a named range. As mentioned in Problem 3, when you move the upper left or lower right corner of a named range, the new cell that corner was moved to becomes the new upper left or lower right cell of the named range. That means the new range includes new cells and no longer includes other cells. Naturally, the formula will return a different answer.

To correct this mistake, take the cell you just moved and put it back in its original location, and then copy it to the new location. Do a /**R**ange Erase on the original cell if you like.

After a Move or Copy command, check all formulas to ensure that they're still accurate, and check named ranges to make sure that the names still apply to the proper cells.

Problem 5:

After the Copy command, a formula has weird cell references

This situation is unique to the Copy command. It also happens most often when you copy in cells close to the edge of the worksheet area, the so-called border cells.

Copying a formula causes its relative cell references to be adjusted for the new location. If the formula in A3 adds A2 and A1, copying it to A1 will cause it to add the two cells above it.

A Suggestion of Thumb

This suggestion is really not a rule of thumb because every situation is different. When using the Move and Copy commands around formulas, however, here's some good general advice:

- Move a formula if you don't want the answer to change when it gets to its new cell

- Copy the formula if you want it to refer to new cells after it gets to the new cell

- Copy to and from cells which are referred to in formulas

You're saying there are no cells above it, right? Correct. So the formula refers to the two cells at the very bottom of the column, cells A8192 and A8191.

An @SUM formula copied too close to the boundary cells gives much more serious results. Imagine a formula in A3, which is @SUM(A1..A2). Copy the formula to A2. Now the formula looks like @SUM(A1..A8192). It includes every cell in column A now that the relative cell references are changed, and the formula is circular. Chapters 1 and 13 describe CIRCular formulas in detail. Chapter 13 also provides more information about the problems associated with copying too close to boundaries.

If you make the mistake of copying too close to boundaries, try Undo first. If that's not possible, copy the formula back to where it was before the copy. If it has to be relocated close to the boundary cells, consider editing the formula after it gets there. Press F2 (Edit) with the cell pointer in the formula cell and change the necessary cell references.

Problem 6:
You try to copy one cell to several cells but only the first row of the TO range received data

You highlighted more than the one cell when you were asked to enter the range you're copying from. Users often highlight the cell they want to copy and some empty cells below it when the prompt says Copy what?. Then, when they highlight the cells they want to copy to, only the first cell in the TO range has data because the empty cells they highlighted in the FROM range were copied to the cells below that top cell.

Go back to the cell(s) you wanted to copy and start the command again. This time be careful about what you highlight when the prompt says Copy what?. Highlight *only* the cells you want to copy.

Problem 7:
You move data to a distant range and it disappears

This situation is unique to Move. Students sometimes enter data and move it several times because they don't understand the Move command and think they've lost their data. For example, enter your name in cell A1 and then move it to cell EA1. The cell pointer stays in cell A1 (it always goes back to the cell you were in before you invoked the command) but your name has disappeared. Think about it for a second and you'll realize that this is exactly what's supposed to happen. Move means that the data is no longer in the original cell. Of course, if you can't see the place the data was moved to it might appear to have been lost.

There is no solution to this problem because it really isn't a problem; it's a misunderstanding of the Move command. Rest assured that when you move data, it will disappear from its original cell and end up in its new cell. Go to the new cell to ensure that it got there and then, reassured, continue with your work.

Problem 8:
When you copy a range to a new range with a different format, you're disappointed that the numbers don't get the new format

Local formats are copied along with the data. If the FROM range had no format and you copy to a range formatted for currency, hoping that the numbers will look like money when they get there, you're out of luck. The absence of format will be copied to the new cells with the data you're copying.

Out of Order

It's possible, and maybe more convenient, to highlight the FROM range before you start the Copy or Move commands. To highlight a range with the mouse, hold the left button down, or press F4 (ABS), and highlight a range with the arrow keys. When you start the Move or Copy command, it uses the highlighted range for the Copy what? part of the command and skips right to the To where? prompt.

Protection status is also copied. If you copy an unprotected range to a range that is protected, and you assume that no one will be able to change or erase your data, you might have a nasty surprise.

After copying or moving data, you'll have to format or change the protection status of the data in the new range if it isn't correct.

Problem 9:
You use Copy and all Wysiwyg formats, except lines, are copied with the data

This is another difference between the Move and the Copy commands. Move will move all Wysiwyg formats including lines, and Copy will copy all formats except lines. To ensure that the lines get to the new range with everything else, use the /Copy command to get the data to the new cells, then use the :Special Copy command. This command copies all Wysiwyg formats to the new range.

A Last Word on Copying and Moving

The Copy and Move commands seem harder to learn for new users than many other commands. Even when the keystrokes are mastered, there is always something new to be learned and some new mistake to be made in executing them. Your best bet is to practice the keystrokes until they come naturally. Try both Move and Copy, and try them on both single cells and ranges.

What To Do When...

You Can't Enter or Edit Data

Entering data into cells is a basic skill in 1-2-3, but that doesn't mean it's always easy. Typing a cell entry and getting beeped is a bit like bumping into a wall. It's surprising and frustrating and impedes progress.

In this chapter, you explore the reasons 1-2-3 refuses to accept your data.

Your First Data

The first thing anyone does when learning 1-2-3 is enter data in a cell. The task is fairly easy: you type the data and press Enter (or an arrow key). Sometimes, however, when you type something and press Enter, your computer beeps and the indicator in the upper right corner of the screen changes to EDIT. This indicates that the entry you typed is unacceptable.

When you type something, press Enter, and get an error message, you may have no idea what's going on. Fortunately, you'll face this problem only on rare occasions. Some of those times are discussed in this section.

The Value of a Label

Before looking at any data-entry problems you might encounter, you need to understand what happens when you type your data. The moment you type the first character, 1-2-3 decides whether it is a label or a value. There is a big difference. Following is a list of differences between labels and values:

- Labels can spill out of a cell to the right as far as necessary to display everything you type (up to 240 characters).

- Values only fill the cell left to right. If the values are too big for the cell, they will appear as stars.

- Labels can be anything you type.

- Values must be formulas or numbers. They can't be numbers followed by letters.

- Values can be used in numerical formulas, labels can't. All labels have a value of zero.

- If there is something in the cell to the right of a long label, only part of the label will be visible.

- You either see all of a value or you see stars.

- Values can be numerically formatted, labels cannot.

- Labels can be realigned in a cell, which means that they can be aligned with the right or left side of the cell or centered in it.

- Values cannot be aligned in a cell.

As you can see, when 1-2-3 makes this decision about what you're typing, it's an important one. If the first character you type is a number, you're typing a value. If the first character you type is a letter, you're typing a label. Usually it's fine to let 1-2-3 decide what the entry is, but at other times you need to take control. The following sections discuss some of those times.

Occasionally, it's best to change a value to a label, and those instances are discussed later in this section. To change a value to a label, you must type a label prefix before you type the cell entry. There are three label prefixes: an apostrophe ('), which places a label in the left side of a cell; a quotation mark ("), which places the label in the right side of the cell; and a caret (^), the Shift+6 key, which centers a label in the cell. By using a label prefix, you accomplish two things: you change a value into a label, and you position it in the cell.

Don't put a label prefix in front of a real value, though; it is given a value of zero so it can't be used in calculations.

10 Do's and Don'ts When Entering Data

1. *Do* put the cell pointer in the cell where you want the data to be.

2. *Don't* try typing commas or dollar signs in values; they'll be ignored.

3. *Do* use label prefixes in front of ZIP codes, telephone numbers, and other numbers that are really labels.

4. *Don't* type letters after you start typing numbers in a cell entry.

5. *Do* use the F2 key to edit data rather than typing the entire cell entry again.

6. *Don't* put label prefixes in front of numbers you want to use in formulas.

7. *Do* widen columns if you plan to use them for long numbers.

8. *Don't* start values with spaces, or put spaces anywhere in values.

9. *Do* start formulas with a plus sign if they would otherwise start with a letter.

10. *Don't* write your entire life history in a single cell unless your entire life history can be written in 240 characters or less. That is the maximum number of characters a cell can accept.

Problem 1:
You try to enter data in a cell and you get beeped, and an error message appears that says Protected cell

Protection is a condition you can put on your worksheet that makes it impossible for anyone to enter or change data in cells. Protection is turned on with /Worksheet Global Protection Enable. After that command is executed, every cell has an "invisible protective shield."

That doesn't help if you want to enter data. The solution is to unprotect the cells in which you want to enter data.

To unprotect just the cells in which you want to work, use /Range Unprotect and highlight the proper cells. If you want to unprotect the whole worksheet, use /Worksheet Global Protection Disable.

> **I Can't Remember a Thing**
>
> Don't use /Range Unprotect on your entire worksheet. To make it possible to enter data, use /Worksheet Global Protection Disable. The difference? The range command puts a unique characteristic in every cell, which takes up a lot of memory. Worksheet Global Protection Disable doesn't use up memory. Use /Range Protect only on cells you specifically want to use for data entry.

Problem 2:
You type a cell entry and you get beeped

Chances are that you typed numbers followed by letters. An example might be a street address, such as 44 College Ave. As soon as you type the first 4, 1-2-3 decides you're typing a value. However, as soon as you type the first letter, 1-2-3 no longer recognizes the entry as a value and becomes confused. If you were a computer and you were confused, you would beep too.

Anytime you type numbers followed by letters, expect a beep unless you use label prefixes. This situation is true of such cell entries as street addresses, insurance policy numbers, and part numbers.

Problem 3:
You type a cell entry and nothing happens. You can't do anything.

Very possibly the computer has locked up. This situation is discussed in detail in Chapter 4, "Dealing with Disaster When It Strikes." In short, this problem is the worst. There is little you can do except restart your computer.

Don't be too hasty, though. If your computer has locked up, you don't have to rush to restart it. Give the computer a little time; you might have issued a command that needs a few seconds to execute. Let it run its course, then try entering data. If nothing happens, then reboot the computer.

Problem 4:
You try entering a formula and get beeped when you press enter

You have to get the formula exactly right before 1-2-3 will accept it. When you enter an invalid formula, 1-2-3 beeps and puts you in the EDIT mode (you see the word EDIT in the upper right corner of the screen). If you don't know how to fix the formula, press Esc, and then check the documentation or use the Help feature. Just type the beginning of the formula with which you need help, @SUM for example, and then press F1 (Help) and you'll get on-line help with that formula. You must type the formula correctly before the Enter key will work.

Point to It

When you write a formula, you must include the range the formula is to act on. You can do this two ways: type every character, keystroke by keystroke, or use pointing. With the pointing method, start the formula by typing @SUM and an open parenthesis. Now, instead of typing the cell addresses, use the arrow key to move to one of the end cells in the range. Anchor the cell pointer there with the period key, and highlight to the other end of the range. Now, type the closed parenthesis and press Enter. The formula is written. This *pointing* method is better because it forces 1-2-3 to supply the argument and removes the possibility that you'll make a mistake.

What did you do wrong? Although there are lots of ways to make mistakes with formulas, the most common is to add spaces. Spelling a function wrong is not a good idea, either. For example, the @SUM formula cannot be @ SUM (with a space) and it can't be @SUB. Many formulas require arguments—the information inside the parentheses, such as the range in @SUM(A1..B5). Type an invalid argument and 1-2-3 is not happy. Forget a parenthesis and, you guessed it, BEEP! For every open parenthesis there must be a closed parenthesis.

Label It

Sometimes writing a formula takes a lot of time and study, but until you get it right you can't enter it into the cell. There is a way around this problem. It's not a final solution, but it does allow you to enter the formula. Put a label prefix in front of the formula. You can enter it even if it's wrong. Of course, it won't calculate anything because it's a label, but at least it's entered. Now you can edit it and see if it works by removing the label prefix. If it works, great. If it doesn't, put a label prefix at the beginning, enter it into the cell, and keep on editing until it works.

Some good advice here is to check the documentation or the Help system for the exact syntax (the form) of the command. To use Help, start typing the formula and then press F1 (Help). You'll see a screen full of helpful information about that formula.

Problem 5:
You type a value and 1-2-3 won't accept it, and you didn't type any letters, either

No, but you might have typed a space or two. Be sure when you type a

Not Now

When you're typing the value is not the time to add commas or dollar signs. They will be ignored by 1-2-3. The way to add these to values is with the format commands. Use /Worksheet Global Format or /Range Format, and then select the proper format. For dollar signs, use currency; to put commas in numbers, use the comma format.

value that you don't type any spaces in or after the number.

Problem 6:
You enter some values, write a formula to sum them, but you get zero

There are three possible causes here. One is that you wrote the formula wrong and it's adding the wrong cells. Press F2 (Edit) and correct the mistake.

The other two possibilities are that you typed either a space or a label prefix at the beginning of the value that made it a label.

Go to the value cells and press F2 (Edit). Press the Home key to move the cursor to the first character in the value. Is it a number? It should be. If it's not, press the Delete key to delete any unwanted characters.

Problem 7:
You type a fine formula (A1+A2 for example) hoping for an answer, but in the cell you get A1+A2

The reason is simple. As soon as you typed the first A, 1-2-3 recognized what you were typing. It's a label. Labels can't do math. You need to trick 1-2-3 into thinking you typed a value. To do that, type a plus sign before a formula that would otherwise begin with a letter.

Press the F2 (Edit) key, then the Home key to move to the left end of the formula. Delete the label prefix, probably an apostrophe. Type a + (plus sign) and then press Enter.

Problem 8:
You type a bunch of numbers into a cell and press Enter. The numbers don't look at all the way you want them to.

Some numbers are really labels. Your phone number, your ZIP code, your insurance policy number, and your Social Security number are examples. Try typing your phone number into a cell with the dash.

The result is not what you expected at all, because 1-2-3 sees it as a subtraction problem. The number 555-1212 gives -657 because 1-2-3 subtracted 1212 from 555.

Type a ZIP code that begins with a zero and the zero is lost. 1-2-3 automatically removes unnecessary zeros.

A date entered as 12/25/93 is not a date, it's a division problem. You get a decimal.

How do you get around this? You type a label prefix in front of a number that is really a value, and it will look just the way you typed it. For example, type

    '12/25/93

and in the cell you'll see 12/25/93, not 0.005161.

Problem 9:
You enter data in a cell and don't get beeped, but you can't see the data

You probably tried to enter data in the same range as a graph. You can add a blank graph to a range, and then type numbers in that range; the numbers won't be visible. Even a graph that you can see has edges that extend beyond the visible part of the graph. Put data there and it is invisible.

To see whether the current cell has a graph, look in the control panel. If a graph is there, the panel

> **You Don't Look Right**
>
> When you enter a value in a range and the value doesn't look right, the cell may have been formatted. Imagine entering the number 500 into a cell formatted for percent. You would see 50000%. If the cell is formatted with the text format, you'll see the formula rather than the answer. If the +/– format is in place, watch out. You get a bunch of plus or minus signs or stars. You need to reformat to change the appearance of the number.

will say so after the cell address. You'll see A11: {Graph Blank or Current or Name} in the top part of the screen. If this is the case, move the data to another cell.

You might also have entered data into a cell that has been formatted as hidden. The control panel will tell you whether the cell has a hidden format. If it does, the letter *H* in parentheses appears after the cell address. Use /Range Format Reset to remove this format, and you'll be able to see your data.

A Last Word on Data Entry

As you can see, this business of data entry is not as simple as it seems. The most important points to remember are the differences between labels and values and making those differences work for you.

Your Data Does a Disappearing Act

The bottom drops out of your day when your worksheet is progressing nicely and then . . . suddenly the data is gone. The program is still working, but there's no data. Where is it, and how do you get it back? This chapter has some answers.

Cells, Ranges, and Data

Data is entered one cell at a time. Where the cell pointer is determines where the data will go. You type data you want to enter into a
cell, press Enter or an arrow key, and the data is in the cell.

Data can be removed one cell at a time, too. What's scary is that it
can also be removed from several cells or from the entire worksheet
at once. What's even scarier is that it can happen by accident.

Sometimes the data isn't really gone, it's just not visible. In any case,
the trick is getting it back on-screen. This chapter covers the ways
data can be erased and the ways it can seem to be erased but still be
there. You also learn some pointers about how to prevent data loss
and ways to get it back.

Data Ins and Outs

To get data into a cell you usually type it. There are other ways, too.
One way is to issue the /Data Fill command, which allows you to fill
a specified range with numbers. The data starts with any number you
choose. You set the difference between each number and the next,
and you specify the last number.

You can also do a /File Combine, which calls data from other
worksheets saved on disk and places it in the current worksheet.

Whenever data enters a cell, existing cell contents are lost. For
example, if you're feeling a bit groggy after a long session and you
aren't watching what you're doing, you can easily enter data into a
cell that already has data. Doing a /Data Fill or a /File Combine over
a range also can cause loss of data. So, data in *can* mean data out.

Sometimes, however, you want to erase data. The easiest way to erase one cell is to go to the cell and press Delete. To clear more than one cell, use the /Range Erase command. First highlight carefully all the cells you want to erase, and then press Enter. To clear the entire worksheet off the screen (save it first!) use /Worksheet Erase

The best insurance you have at your disposal is the Undo feature. Make sure it's on, and then work with the added protection of being able to undo your last action. You know it's on when a "flag" appears at the bottom of the screen with the word UNDO in it. Check Chapter 8 for more information about turning on Undo.

Remember, you can only undo one action at a time and it must be the last thing you did before using Undo. In other words, when you make a mistake, your next move should be to use Undo. Don't feel pressured to rush into trying every key on the keyboard to fix the problem; it'll only make things worse, and you won't be able to use Undo.

10 Do's and Don'ts To Avoid Data Loss

1. *Do* save early and often.

2. *Don't* retrieve a new worksheet until you've saved the one currently on-screen.

3. *Do* use the Hidden format carefully.

4. *Don't* confuse the /Worksheet Delete command with /Range Erase.

5. *Do* have Undo on if at all possible.

6. *Don't* confuse /Worksheet Erase and /Range Erase.

7. *Do* remember that you can select a command only from the top menu line. When you call up a menu, pick an item from the top line only.

8. *Don't* answer screen prompts hastily. The prompt `Worksheet changes not saved, retrieve anyway? No Yes` is trying to tell you something.

9. *Do* check your worksheet occasionally to ensure that all data is intact.

10. *Don't* whack away madly at the keyboard hoping that some random set of keystrokes will fix the problem.

Dealing with Disappearing Data

With sufficient care, unscheduled data loss can be avoided. Of course, with sufficient care nothing in the world would ever go wrong. Problems do occur, but knowing how to enter and delete data and use the commands correctly will make things go a lot smoother.

Problem 1:
You delete data in a cell, but you want it back

Data in a cell is deleted in one of three ways. You either enter new data in the cell, press the Delete key, or use /Range Erase on the one cell.

The best way to get your data back is to undo it, by pressing Alt+F4. (Of course, you need to have the Undo feature enabled for this to work.) You can't use Undo if the deletion was not the last thing you did or if Undo isn't on. Sorry, but the only alternative is to reenter the data.

Problem 2:
You accidentally delete data in a range

You probably used /Range Erase and highlighted more cells than you wanted to. Once again, you can get the data back by using the Undo key or by reentering the data. If it's a lot of data and reentering it is going to be time-consuming, consider retrieving the same file from the disk and continuing from there. This situation is yet another argument for saving often.

Problem 3:
You delete all the data from an entire row or column

Many users forget the real result of using the /Worksheet Delete Row or Column command. Keep in mind that when you use this command, it takes place in the row or column where the cell pointer is located; the entire column is deleted along with the data in it. If you highlight to the side or up and down, more rows and columns are sacrificed. It is not possible to delete part of a column or row by using this command. Use /Range Erase if you want to delete just data.

It also happens frequently that people delete a row when they mean to delete a column, or vice versa. Whatever happens, the data from border to shining border is gone, along with the row or column it was in. All rows below the deleted one shift up one, and a new blank row appears in row 8192. All columns to the right of the deleted one shift to the left, and a new empty column is placed in column IV.

The problem, of course, is getting the data back. Don't be surprised if I suggest Undo. That is the quickest and most efficient solution. Failing that, you have to leave the cell pointer in the row or column where it ended up after the delete and perform a /Worksheet Insert Column or Row. This action places a new blank column or row where you need it. Highlighting downward or to the right allows you to insert more than one column or row.

The Insert command pushes data down or to the right, and empty columns at the edge of the worksheet are pushed out into space. If there is data at the edge of the worksheet, an error message appears saying Worksheet Full.

Don't Get Too Pushy!

While you're lurking about in the worksheet menu, remember that using /Worksheet Insert Row or Column to insert a large number of rows or columns may shove data off the screen. Naturally, it is not gone, it's just moved. Your worksheet is now spread over a larger area because of the new (and so far empty) columns or rows, which means that existing data is certainly going to be affected.

After the new row or column is inserted, data entry or reentry is your next job. Naturally, if you saved your work recently, this situation can be minimized. Retrieve the file and hope that little catch-up work is necessary.

Problem 4:
You delete an entire worksheet

This happens when you do one of two things. Perhaps you retrieved a new file and the work on-screen disappears because it's replaced by the new file. Or, maybe you used /Worksheet Erase and your work is history.

It's easy to confuse the meaning of /Range Erase and /Worksheet Erase. Range Erase deletes data from a range, and Worksheet Erase takes the whole worksheet off the screen.

Once again, you have three choices. First, try Undo. Second, hope you saved it recently and retrieve it. Your last choice, I hate to say, is to start all over entering data.

What'd He Say?

One big difference between /Range Erase and /Worksheet Erase is a couple of extra steps in /Worksheet Erase. A prompt appears at the top of the screen confirming that you do indeed want to erase all data. You have to answer by selecting Yes or No. If you haven't saved the current work, another prompt appears telling you that you haven't saved the changes to the worksheet, do you REALLY want to erase. Unfortunately the common response to such prompts is to shoot first and ask questions later—answer with a "Yes" and then wonder what the prompt said. Goodbye data.

When you execute /File Retrieve, 1-2-3 checks to see if you've saved the work currently visible. If not, it prompts you with a Yes/No question, Worksheet Changes Not Saved! Retrieve anyway? If you answer "Yes" and retrieve a new file, the data currently on the screen will be lost.

Problem 5:
You suddenly dump 1-2-3 and are back at DOS

Don't panic. If you did this with a single keystroke, here's what you probably did. You know that to invoke a command in 1-2-3 you press the slash key to call up the commands, and then you select the command you want. Selection can be done in two ways: highlight the proper word and press Enter, or press the first letter of the command you want. There's the problem. If you're not careful you'll make a mistake that will put your heart in your throat.

You probably wanted to save your file, so you called up the menu. You know that Save begins with an *S* so you pressed that letter.

There's the mistake. You should have pressed F for File *first* and then S for Save. Always select a command from the current top row.

What did that *S* do? It invoked a command called System. The purpose of the **System** command is to suspend 1-2-3 temporarily to allow you to issue

DOS commands. It looks for all the world as though you suddenly exited from 1-2-3, but you didn't. Hands off the keyboard and read the screen. It says Type Exit and Press Enter to Return to 1-2-3. Do that and you're back in 1-2-3, data undamaged. Don't type 123 at the DOS prompt, you don't want to start a new session. And whatever you do, don't reboot your computer, or the data *will* be lost.

Problem 6:
You use a command, and the screen is filled with new information

Some of the commands you might select, whether by accident or on purpose, call boxes to the screen that either show you settings for that command or enable you to make selections about that command. If these boxes show you settings, they are called *settings sheets*. If these boxes allow you to make selections, they are called *dialog boxes*. A good example of a settings sheet or dialog box is the Graph command. If you press / and then G for Graph, your data disappears simply because a settings sheet appeared over the data. Just press Esc or Ctrl +Break to exit from the menu and return to the READY mode if you really want to see your data. Or, continue with the menu, assured that your data awaits you at the end of the command.

Problem 7:
You press a key to move to a different cell and all data disappears

It is quite possible that you lost your data because you lost your way. It's easy to do if you don't watch what keys you press as you navigate around the worksheet. Here's what to watch out for.

On your way to press the Insert, Delete, or Home key, you might accidentally press the End key. Although you may not notice it, the END flag appears at the bottom of the screen. Now, if you press one of the arrow keys or the Home key, the cell pointer might move far from where you want it to be. This happens because the End key moves the cell pointer in the direction of the arrow key you pressed, to the last cell that is a border between full and empty cells. Sometimes the cell pointer moves clear to the edge of the worksheet. You could end up in row 8192 or column IV. The antidote here is to press F5 and then the address of the cell where your data is located. The Home key might also do it if your data is at or near cell A1.

> ### Setting the Settings Sheets
>
> When you see a settings sheet on-screen, you can use the menu to change items. Another way is to press F2, which activates the sheet. You can tell that the sheet is active because some of the letters become brighter. Now you can press the letter of the item you want to change and edit the settings sheet. This action enables you to ignore the menu.
>
> The mouse can also be used to edit the settings sheet. For example, place the mouse pointer on the item you want to change, click, and type in your changes.

Other cursor movement keys that can raise your temperature are PgUp, PgDn, and Tab. These are fine keys and very useful, but if you didn't intend to move up, down, or to the right one whole screen, you might think your data went on vacation.

Here are the best ways to return to your data:

- Press Home to move to cell A1 (that's probably where your data starts)

- Press F5 (Goto) and then type the cell address or range name you want to go to

- If you pressed PgDn, press PgUp

- If you pressed Tab, press Shift+Tab

Problem 8:
You play hide-and-seek with your data, but now you can't find it

Your data is still where it was, you just can't see it. 1-2-3 has three commands that allow you to hide data. One of these commands is /Worksheet Global Format Hidden. When you use this command, the contents of every cell may disappear. Only cells you formatted with /Range Format will remain visible. To reverse this problem, use Undo or select /Worksheet Global Format and pick any other format. The General format means that all cells will be displayed without any formatting.

Another way to hide cells is to use /Range Format Hidden. This command hides the cells you highlight, even cells with labels in them. Fix this problem by using Undo or /Range Format and pick any other format. The Reset option removes all range formatting from the highlighted cells.

The /Worksheet Column Hide command allows highlighted columns to be hidden from view. The data is still there, and formulas that refer to cells in the hidden columns still work, you just can't see the column. If you print a range that includes the hidden columns, the columns will not print.

Don't Overdo It

When you want to hide or redisplay a bunch of columns, you don't have to highlight the entire column, top to bottom. As long as one cell in the column is highlighted, you can do the job just fine.

This command is usually used to hide sensitive data. It is also useful for getting two distant columns closer together, and it neatens up the display by hiding columns of unimportant data you don't need to see.

If you want to see the data, the way to get it back on-screen is to use /Worksheet Column Display. All the hidden columns reappear, and if you look up the frame, you'll see that the hidden columns have an asterisk next to the column letter. Highlight all the columns you want to redisplay and press Enter. They're back.

Problem 9:
You reformat numbers, now the stars are out

Sometimes data doesn't exactly disappear, it just changes its appearance into something useless, like stars. This happens when a value is reformatted and winds up too big for a cell. 1-2-3 won't display part of a value if the whole number cannot be seen in the cell; instead, stars appear indicating that the number is too big for the current column width. To change the stars back into values, either reformat the values or widen the column.

1-2-3 has three commands for widening columns. Which one you select depends on how many columns you want to widen. You can widen one, all, or several columns. Use the following table:

To widen one column	Choose **Worksheet Column Set-Width** from either the main menu or the Wysiwyg menu.
To widen all columns	Choose **/Worksheet Global Column-Width** from the menu.
To widen some columns	Choose **/Worksheet Column Column-Range Set-Width** from the menu, and highlight the columns you want to affect. You also can use **:Worksheet Column Set-Width** from the Wysiwyg menu, and then highlight the columns to be widened.

Widen the column(s) by either typing the desired width or pressing the right arrow to widen the column(s) one character at a time. Finally, press Enter to complete the command.

Problem 10:
You use Wysiwyg to change colors and wind up with no data

Colors are changed in two ways. You can use the :Display Colors Background or Text menu, or the :Format Colors Background or Text menu. The Display menu changes colors in the whole worksheet; the Format menu affects only a range or a cell. In either case, be sure that the two colors you choose are different.

Your favorite color may look great on your walls, but don't use that color for text and background. Your data will disappear until you change the background or text color to something different. Be sure the new color you choose is really different from the other color in the cell. For example, if your background color is dark blue, don't use black letters. Not only will the cell be rather gloomy, it also will be hard to read.

Problem 11:
You use the Wysiwyg shade command, now you can't see your data

To make a cell or range stand out from the others, you can apply shading to it using the /Format Shade command. Shading comes in three varieties: light, dark, and solid. Solid shading fills a cell or range with a solid color and nothing can be seen through it.

Depending on the size of the font you used and the color of the cell, even light or dark shade may make your data hard to read or make it nearly invisible.

So, be careful when you use shading. Try :Format Shade

Put It on Paper

What will cells look like when they're printed? Often the data on paper looks a lot different from the data on-screen. Here are two suggestions for making sure that your printout will please. First, if you have a color monitor and the printer is black only, change your display to black and white to see how the data looks. Use :Display Mode B&W. Now, while you're in black-and-white mode, highlight the print range and do a :Print Preview. Check to see that the Wysiwyg formats you piled up in a cell don't obliterate the data.

and Light or Dark and highlight your cells; then be sure you can read them. If you can't, use :Format Shade Clear.

Problem 12:
You place a graph over your data, now you can't see the data

The Wysiwyg menu contains the commands you use to place a graph in your worksheet. The sequence is :Graph Add; then pick the type of graph you want to place in the worksheet, highlight the range in which the graph is to be displayed, and press Enter. If you high-lighted a range containing data, the data will be hidden behind the graph.

You can remove the graph or move it. You can remove the graph by putting the cell pointer in any cell in which the graph was placed and selecting :Graph Remove, and then pressing Enter.

To move the graph, again place the cell pointer in the range occupied by the graph, select :Graph Settings Range, press Enter, high-light the new range for the graph (not over data this time, please), and press Enter.

Another option, if you insist on keeping the graph and data in the same place, is to make the graph transparent. Put your cell pointer in the graph and execute :Graph Settings Opaque No. Now data behind the graph will show between the parts of the graph.

A Last Word on Data

Slow and steady wins the day. It is usually hastiness in executing commands that causes data to disappear. It is also hastiness in trying to correct the problem that makes it unsolvable. Knowledge is power. Knowing what particular commands do will help you avoid the nasty surprises that data loss can bring.

What To Do When. . .

Your Data Won't Sort

The name *1-2-3* was chosen for a reason. Besides spreadsheet and graphics capabilities, the program also offers a database. Like any database program, the 1-2-3 database can be queried and sorted. As with any database, it is also possible to make little mistakes and to misunderstand some of the steps. This chapter provides some useful information about the 1-2-3 database.

A Quick Lesson on Using 1-2-3 as a Database

When you create a database in 1-2-3, you have to play by the rules or you are courting disaster (or at least disappointment). First, arrange your data in columns. For example, if you wanted to make your mailing list a database, you might put the last name of each person in the first column, the first name in the second column, the street address in the third, and so forth.

At the top of each column, insert a column title, and don't skip any lines after the title or in the database itself. Skipping lines can result in corrupted sorting and queries. Because there are 8192 rows, and the top row is titles, you can have a total of 8191 records.

Learning the Terms

To understand how databases work, you have to understand a couple of database terms. *Records* are the information contained in each row. For example, in the name and address database, each row has a name, address, and phone number. That's one record.

The columns contain *fields*. Each field is a piece of information about the records. In the name and address database, for example, last name, first name, street address, and so forth are fields.

The individual entries for each field in each record are the *data*. To create a database, you enter the data for each person in a row, one record per row, one field per column. You don't have to put the data in alphabetical or numerical order, 1-2-3 will do that for you.

Putting Yourself in Command

After the database is complete, you can use two commands to rearrange the data: **Sort** and **Query**.

Sort puts your database in any order you want. You can put your address list in alphabetical order by last name, by state, by street address, or by any other field you choose. You can also decide whether the sort order is ascending or descending. *Ascending* means that data will be arranged from A to Z, or from lowest to highest number. *Descending* means the opposite. The records will be arranged from Z to A or from highest to lowest number.

Query means that you want the program to look through your database and locate certain records that meet your criteria. Query has several choices: **Find, Extract, Unique,** and **Delete.**

Find sends the cell pointer to the first record in the database that meets your criteria. **Extract** takes all records that meet the criteria and puts them in a separate place. **Unique** is like Extract but with one change. It copies records to the output range, but places duplicates in the output range only once. **Delete** removes from the database any records that meet your criteria.

Be sure you save before you use any of these commands, just in case you make a mistake. Unless Undo is on, you can make a mess out of a database with Sort or Query. It's good to know the original list is stored safely on disk.

How To Do What You Need To Do

The following sections provide a quick course in dealing with 1-2-3 database operations.

Sorting Data

To put your database in order, choose /Data Sort. You now have to highlight one range and designate two sort keys. The data range is *all* your database from left to right and from top to bottom—except for the top row, the titles.

The next step is to decide the primary and secondary keys. The *primary key* is the column that determines the order of the database. The *secondary key* breaks ties. For example, if you have several people in your database named Snurd and you want to sort by last name, the primary key puts last names in order, and the secondary key puts the Snurds in alphabetical order by first name.

To determine the primary and secondary keys, place the cell pointer anywhere in the proper column and press Enter. You don't have to highlight the entire column when choosing keys. After you determine the key, you have to choose A or D to tell 1-2-3 whether the sort will be ascending or descending.

Watch the **Reset** command. It immediately clears all your ranges and you'll have to repeat all the commands. It's a fine command when you want to sort another database—all ranges are cleared immediately. If you choose **Reset** accidentally, however, you have some catching up to do. Save the file before sorting, just in case you make a mistake, and then choose **Go**. In a flash, your database is in the order you chose.

Querying the Database

To query a database, you must highlight the following ranges:

- *Input*—This range covers the entire database including the titles at the top of the columns.

- *Criteria*—This range is normally two rows. The top row must have EXACTLY the same titles as the input range. You type your criteria in the second row.

- *Output*—This range is one row. In that row, put the column titles EXACTLY as they appear at the top of the database and in the criteria range.

Again, watch out for the **Reset** command. Your hard work can be undone easily in a single keystroke.

After the three ranges are entered, go to the second row of the criteria range and type the criteria you want to use to query the database. For example, to locate all the records of people from Kentucky, type Kentucky under the column title for state. To find each record, choose /Data Find. The highlight goes to the first record that meets your criteria. After that, each time you press Enter the cell pointer goes to the next record.

After you highlight the last record, you get an error message on-screen telling you that you've found the last record from Kentucky. Press Enter to clear the message. To find records from another state, type the name of the state in the cell where you entered Kentucky. You need not reenter the menu—the F7 (Query) key will execute the last query command you chose through the menu. Now you'll find records for this new state.

To extract records, use the menu and choose /Data Query Extract. Look in the output range and you'll see all the records for the state you typed. Change the state, press F7, and the old records are deleted from the output range and a new set is added.

Sounds Simple. What Can Go Wrong?

A couple of things can go wrong if you're not careful. The first is not highlighting exactly what you mean to highlight when you're designating ranges. Be sure you include all data you want to include, but don't include any extra cells, rows, or columns, and don't highlight more rows in the criteria range than you need to.

Be sure you enter all data in one field as either a value or a label. For example, if you're entering department numbers, be sure that all of them are entered either as values or as labels.

Type criteria exactly as you want them; this is not a time for creativity or variation.

10 Do's and Don'ts When Using 1-2-3 as a Database

1. *Do* put each type of data (field) in a separate column.

2. *Don't* skip lines as you enter data.

3. *Do* put column titles at the top of each column.

4. *Don't* include the title row in the database range when you sort.

5. *Do* include the title row in the database when you query.

6. *Don't* put data in cells below the query output range.

7. *Do* save your work before you sort, in case you make a mistake.

8. *Don't* include blank rows in the query criteria range.

9. *Do* ensure that you highlight the entire database as the data range when you sort.

10. *Don't* forget to expand the data range for Sort or the input range for Query when you add data to your database. New data isn't automatically included.

How To Deal with Database Problems

Plenty can go wrong if you don't follow instructions to the letter. Keep the do's and don'ts in mind and refer to the problems that follow when things go awry.

Problem 1:
You try to sort a database and only one or two columns are sorted

This problem is caused by forgetting to highlight the whole database before you sort. For example, imagine that you want to sort a name and address database by last name (primary key) and first name (secondary key). If, by accident, you highlight just those two columns when you're supposed to highlight the data range, only those two columns will sort. When the sort is done, the names will be in alphabetical order all right. But, because only the names were sorted, they'll be in rows with someone else's phone number and address. Highlight the whole database so that when the names go to new rows, they take their other data with them.

> ### Leave Me Out of This
>
> When you highlight the data range, don't include the title row. Also, don't highlight any blank rows at the bottom. If you do, they'll be sorted with the database. If column A has *Last Name* as a title, after you sort you'll find the words *Last Name* down in the database after Lassiter and before Lawrence.

This kind of problem shows why you should save before you sort or query. If you can't Undo the sort, you've made a mess of your database. It's a relief when you can retrieve the file from the disk and try again, this time highlighting the entire data range.

Problem 2:

You do a query-extract, but not all records you expect wind up in the output range

The output range must be only one row, and that row must include the column titles from the input range. You might have highlighted several rows for the output range. If you highlight six rows for example, only five records will be put in the output range. (The top row is the titles.) By highlighting just the title row, you let 1-2-3 use as much space as it wants for the data it extracts.

Put Stars in Your State

What if you did enter a state's name several different ways? Is it really necessary, for example, to change all 4,000 records of people from Pennsylvania? No, you have two alternatives.

One is to use a search and replace to correct the variations. An even better solution, however, is to use a *wild card character* in the criterion range. If you used PA, PENNA, PENN, and PENNSYLVANIA in the state column, for example, you can use P* as a criterion. The addition of the asterisk means that 1-2-3 will look for the state in each record that begins with P, and any characters after that letter are acceptable.

Another reason you don't get all the data you want could be that when you entered the data, you did so inconsistently. This situation could happen in the state column, for example, where you might enter the state name in several different ways. If you set RI as your criterion, R.I. or Rhode Island will be ignored. Go to the proper column and make sure that the data is exactly the same as the criterion.

One other possibility is that you added records to the input range but forgot to increase the size of the input range to include the new data. Use /Data Query Input and highlight all data so that the input range is expanded to include all data.

Problem 3:

When you sort, you get numbers first, but you want them at the end of the sort order

By default, when you sort, numbers are sorted first if they're labels and last if they're values. This sorting order applies even when you choose descending sort order.

In the column where you entered street addresses, some entries may be by number and street, such as 625 Main Street, which must be preceded by a label prefix. Other addresses may be by post office box numbers, such as Box 104, which requires no label prefix because 1-2-3 automatically recognizes them as labels. Now, if you sort the street addresses, those that begin with numbers will always appear first.

To change this order, you have to quit 1-2-3 and start the install program. Type install at the DOS prompt. When the install program starts, choose Change Selected Equipment from the menu. Then choose Modify the Current Driver Set, and then Collating Sequence.

At this point you have three choices:

- *ASCII*, which sorts according to the ASCII number of the characters. The ASCII sort order is numbers, capital letters, and then lowercase letters.

- *Numbers last* means that numbers entered as labels appear in sort order after letters.

- *Numbers first*, the default, means that numbers entered as labels appear in sort order before letters.

Be careful in columns where you enter data that is just numbers. If some are labels (they have label prefixes before them) and others are values, the sort order will be labels first and values last. If you enter numbers in a column, be sure they're all values or all labels.

Problem 4:
You do a query and no records appear

Check for the following:

- You typed a criterion in the wrong cell in the criterion range. For example, entering a state name under first name will not extract any data, unless you know someone named Nebraska. Be sure the criterion is entered in the proper column.

- You misspelled the criterion. Spell it the way you did in the Input range. NY as a criterion will not find N.Y.

- The criteria range is only one row—the titles. Expand it to two rows so that it includes the criterion you want.

- The titles in the criteria range are not exactly the same as the titles in the input range. Copy the titles from the top row of the input range to the top row of the criteria and output ranges; then you're sure they're right.

- You did not highlight an output range.

- You typed a criterion for which there are no records.

- Your input range does not include all your data.

- You typed mutually exclusive criteria in the criteria range. That mouthful means you entered more than one criterion in the criteria range. Suppose you enter Catherine in the first name column and NM in the state column. You'll extract all records for people who have the first name Catherine AND who are from New Mexico. If there are none of these, the output range will be empty. You probably want people who are named Catherine OR people from New Mexico. In that case, add another row to the criteria range. In one row under first name enter Catherine. In the other row, under state, Enter NM. Now query.

- You erased a cell in the database or in the criteria range incorrectly. To delete a cell, use the Delete key or /Range Erase. Many people have gotten into the bad habit of clearing a cell with the space bar and the Enter key. You have not emptied a cell when you do this, you've entered a space. A space in the criteria range means that you want to extract records in which a space has been entered in a particular field.

- You have a blank line after the titles in the input range. Use /Worksheet Delete Row to delete the blank row, or move the entire database up one row to get rid of that blank row.

Problem 5:
You type in a criterion and do a query and get all records

Check your criteria range. You'll probably find that it's more than two rows, and one row has no criteria typed in. Here's an example. By accident, when you highlight the criteria range you highlight three rows. In the first row are the column titles. Good. In the first row you typed NJ. Fine. The third row is empty. Bad. The second row tells 1-2-3 to extract all records from New Jersey. The third row, with no criteria typed in, tells 1-2-3 that not only do you want New Jersey records, but also you want all records. You got them.

To correct this problem, be sure you have only as many rows in the criteria range as there are entries. If you type something in one row, make sure only that row and the titles are highlighted.

Problem 6:
You can't figure out how to query on a value field

Suppose that you have a database of employees and you want to query it on salary. To locate all employees with a salary of $35,000, type that figure in the proper cell in the criteria range.

What if you want all employees whose salaries are more than $35,000? In the proper cell in the criteria range, you must write a formula. In the formula, specify the first cell in the input range that has a salary in it. In your database, you might put the word *Salary* in cell D1. In cell D2 should be the first actual salary. So, the formula would be +D2>35000. The formula will evaluate to either a 1 (positive) or a 0 (negative).

This criterion says to 1-2-3: Go to the first salary cell and see whether it's greater than $35,000, then check all the cells below it. Notice that the formula has no dollar sign or comma. When you query the database with this formula, all records that have salaries greater than $35,000 will be found.

Problem 7:
You do a query extract and lose some valuable data

I hope you saved the file before you did your query, or have Undo on. When you do a data query extract, data in the output range is deleted and new data is added. How far down does 1-2-3 delete in the output range? All the way from the title row in the input range to the bottom of the worksheet, row 8192. So, don't enter any data below the output range.

So Long Data

Just in case you weren't paying attention, here is some important news. Any data in rows directly below the Output range to the bottom of the worksheet will be deleted when you do /Data Query Extract. Don't put any data there. Plan your worksheet so all data is placed above or to the side of the output range.

If you did enter data there and you lost it, first use Undo. If that doesn't work, retrieve the file. If you didn't save before the extract, you'll have to reenter the data, this time somewhere other than under the output range.

Remember, if the output range is from cell A10 to G10, every cell from A11 to G8192 will be deleted every time you do a /Data Query Extract.

A Last Word on Databases

1-2-3 can be a powerful database tool, if you follow the rules. When dealing with 1-2-3 database operations, know the rules and follow them exactly. There is no room for creativity here.

The most important thing to remember is that you can really mess up your database with the Sort and Query commands, so save your work before you use these commands. You might also consider saving the same database under a different name so that you always have the original available.

What To Do When...

Your Ranges Are Wrong

CHAPTER TWELVE

As you learned earlier in this book, worksheet commands generally apply to the whole worksheet. What happens, however, when you want to make just one change without affecting the rest of the worksheet? 1-2-3 has a handy tool, the **Range** command, that lets you change one or more ranges in the worksheet without affecting the rest of the worksheet.

To be at home with range commands means that you have to know where mistakes can be made and how to correct them. Keep in mind that a range has to be a rectangular block of cells, no L-shaped group of cells can be highlighted, and two separate groups of cells cannot be a range.

A Change for Your Range

Here's an example of how important the Range command is to you. Imagine doing a payroll in which you use the /Worksheet Global Format command to format all numbers for currency, with two decimal places. In one column, you put the income tax from each employee's home state. If it weren't for the Range command, a state tax rate of five percent would look like $0.05. I'm sure the employees would be thrilled to pay an income tax of five cents, but the appearance of the cells would be misleading. In case you're wondering, any formula referring to those cells would return the correct answer, but the cells themselves would look wrong. The cell looks like five cents, but 1-2-3 uses that value as .05 (the same thing as 5%). Therefore, the formulas using that cell would return the correct answer. The /Range Format command simply changes the way 1-2-3 displays the number in that cell so that the appearance of the number is consistent with its purpose.

Keep in mind that range commands take precedence over global commands, regardless of the order in which the commands are issued. Thus, when you format a range, you override the global format. For example, you might carelessly format a range of numbers and include some extra blank cells. Later, when you enter some numbers in those blank cells, the new numbers may have the wrong format.

Ranges of cells must be highlighted in many areas of the menu besides the /Range commands. Examples are the /Data and both the /Print and :Print (Wysiwyg) menus. In the course of using these commands, you have to highlight a range. Thus, many of the pointers in this chapter apply to these commands as well.

10 Do's and Don'ts for Using the Range Commands

1. *Do* use range commands to make local changes in your worksheet.

2. *Don't* use range commands beyond the active area of the worksheet.

3. *Do* consider highlighting a range before starting the command. Several commands can be executed on the same range when its highlighted.

4. *Don't* use Worksheet commands when you want to change part of the worksheet.

5. *Do* use the Range Name commands to make formula writing and navigation easier.

6. *Don't* be in the middle of a range when you start a Range command. When you're in the middle of a range, highlighting the whole range is much more difficult.

7. *Do* use /**R**ange Erase to empty cells rather than using the space bar and the Enter key.

8. *Don't* forget that the equivalent of /**R**ange is **:**Format in the Wysiwyg menu. Use the **:**Format commands to change part of the worksheet.

9. *Do* remember that some range commands are "sticky." After you've highlighted a range for some commands, that range is remembered and may have to be changed. For example, if you use the Print command and designate a print range, and then reenter the Print command later, the original print range will be highlighted. It is remembered from the previous command.

10. *Don't* spend a lot of time trying to highlight a range that's not a rectangle. It can't be done.

Righting Range Wrongs

Now and then you might run into problems with the range command. The following sections list the more common problems and ways to deal with them.

Problem 1:
You're in the middle of a range and try to highlight left and right, or up and down

Suppose that cells A1 to F1 contain some numbers and you want to format them to look like sums of money (you prefer a 5 to look like $5.00). If you're in cell A3 and start the command, /Range Format Currency 2, you'll encounter the problem. First, you move the highlight to the left to get to cell A1, and then you move the cell pointer to the right. You'll find that A1 and B1 lose the highlight as D1, E1, and so on become selected.

No need to start over. Highlight to one end, and press the period key (.) once. Notice that the winking cursor moves to the other end of the highlighted range. Now you can highlight in the opposite direction.

In general, it is comforting to know that as you highlight, you can jump from one corner of a highlighted range to another corner by pressing the period key repeatedly. Every time you press

Absolutely Easier

An alternative to highlighting the range as part of the command is to highlight the range before you start the command. To do so using the keyboard, press F4 (the Abs key), then highlight a range, press Enter, and start the command. Using the mouse, put the mouse arrow in a corner of the range, hold down the left mouse button, and drag the highlight to the opposite corner of the range. Now start the command. The advantage to this method is that you can perform several commands on the highlighted range. The range stays highlighted until you move the cell pointer.

the period, you move the winking cursor clockwise from corner to corner, and you can highlight outward from that cell to include more cells, rows, or columns in the range.

Usually, it's best to start in a corner of a range before you start the command. This allows you to avoid the extra keystrokes just described.

Problem 2:
You enter the print menu and find a range already highlighted

Print is an example of a sticky range command. Here's how the problem developed: Assume that in an earlier session you printed cells A1 to K50. Now you want to print H1 to K50. Go to cell H1 and start the print command. When you get to the place where you have to highlight the print range, you find that the old range is still highlighted.

Press the Backspace key, which removes the highlight from the old range and returns your cell pointer to its earlier position (in this case, H1). The command is still active, and the cell pointer is in H1. You have to anchor it there and highlight the new range you want to print.

Problem 3:
You type some values and labels, but they don't line up

That's sad, but not something you have to live with. Remember that you can realign the labels but not the values. There is no command to realign values. Also, don't type label prefixes in front of values, because they'll no longer be values.

For the labels, you can use the /Range Label command and then choose **Left**, **Right**, or **Center** depending on where you want the label to be in the cell. Highlight all the offending labels and press Enter. The labels will look much better.

Aligning Long Labels

Here's a trick to keep in mind when you're using Wysiwyg. If you type a long label that spills out of the cell to the right, you can make it spill out in both directions or make it spill out to the left. To make a label spill out in both directions, put two carets (^ ^) in front of it, which centers it on the cell; it spills out in both directions. To make a label spill out to the left, place two quotes in front of it, which aligns the right end of the label with the right side of the cell and makes the label spill out to the left.

Problem 4:

You enter a really long label in a cell but now want it to be in paragraph form

---

Can You Justify That Paragraph?

To make the ragged right side of a paragraph straight (to right-justify it), use the **:Text Align Even** command, which highlights the whole paragraph. The result will be a square block of text with straight left and right sides.

You have two choices: Use the main menu or the Wysiwyg menu; the effect will be the same. Go to the long label and use either **/Range Justify**, or **:Text Reformat**. When the time comes to highlight a range, highlight from left to right to determine how long each line should be in the paragraph you're going to create, then highlight downward far enough to allow all text to be justified.

Problem 5:

You format values in a range, and they look the way you want, but the formulas that use those numbers have the same answers

If you have a range of numbers with lots of decimal places, you might have chosen to format them so that they now only have a couple of visible decimal places. It's easier on the eye. Somewhere else in the worksheet, however, a formula refers to those cells and is still returning loads of decimal places. That's the way it's supposed to work. Formatting a value doesn't change the underlying value, it just makes it look different.

If you want the formula to look like the numbers it's working on, format the cell that holds the formula.

Problem 6:

You try to widen several columns by using /Worksheet Global Column Width but only some widen

The columns didn't widen because they were set previously to a specific width by using /Worksheet Column or Column-Range Set-Width, or :Worksheet Column Set-Width. Columns set previously will not be affected by the global command. If you want one of the previously set columns to conform to this new norm, go to that column and reset it by using /Worksheet Column Reset. If you want to reset several columns, use /Worksheet Column-Range Reset-Width. If you're not sure whether a column has a unique width setting, go to any cell in that column and look in the control panel (upper left corner of the screen). Following the current cell address you'll see the column's width in brackets. For example, you'd see [W 11] if that column were set to a width of 11 characters.

Problem 7:

You try to set a global numerical format but some cells don't change

This problem is similar to the preceding problem. Using /Worksheet Global Format affects every value in the worksheet except values formatted with /Range Format. Again, this feature of the program is deliberate so that some cells can look different from the norm. Look in the control panel and notice that a cell formatted with currency, two decimal places will look like this: A14: (C2). The C2 is the format.

To remove the unique setting, select /Range Format Reset and highlight all cells whose range format you want to remove. Those cells will now have whatever you set with /Worksheet Global Format.

Problem 8:

You hide some data by using /Range Format Hidden. Now you can't see the contents of those cells and you're afraid you'll write over them.

Is It Really Hidden?

Don't trust the hidden format to keep people from seeing the contents of a cell. Putting the cell pointer in a cell and looking at the control panel shows cell contents. So much for security. The main use for this format is to make your spreadsheet neater by hiding cells you don't need to see.

You can see the contents of a hidden cell by placing the cell pointer in that cell and looking at the control panel. To keep cells from accidentally being overwritten or deleted, you need to "protect" them. You can protect cells easier by using /Range Format Reset to remove the hidden format. Then turn global protection on with /Worksheet Global Protection Enable. Now do /Range Unprotect to all cells that you'll want to change later. Finally, rehide the cells that were hidden, and they'll be safe.

Problem 9:

You try using /Range Protect on a range, but you can still change the cell contents

/Range Protect has no effect until you invoke /Worksheet Global Protection Enable. That command protects every cell in the worksheet until you invoke /Range Unprotect on cells you'll want to change. The purpose of /Range Protect is to reverse the Unprotect command you issued earlier.

Problem 10:

You have a number with lots of decimal places in a narrow column, and it is not rounded properly

To correct this problem, use /Range Format Fixed and specify the number of decimal places you want. Now you can be sure that when you narrow the column the number will be properly rounded.

Problem 11:
You enter data in a table, and now you want to reverse rows and columns

Use the /Range Transpose command. This command takes a range and reverses the row and column orientation into a new range (as shown in fig. 8.3). Invoke /Range Transpose and highlight the range you want transposed. Place the cell pointer in the upper left corner of the place where the transposed table is to be, and press Enter.

Problem 12:
You do a /Range Transpose and now the formulas from the original table won't work in the new range

That's the way /Range Transpose works. All formulas are converted to values that command.

If this is a problem, you must go to the cells where you want formulas and write them.

Problem 13:
After filling out a huge worksheet, you find that you made the same data entry mistake all over the place

Lucky for you there's /Range Search. This command will look over an entire range and find or replace any bit of text you want. For example, you might have spelled the name Smith in cells all over the worksheet incorrectly. Perhaps it should be Smythe. Go to the upper left hand corner of the area in which you made the mistake and select /Range Search. You must either type in the range or anchor the cell pointer and highlight all the cells you want to search for this mistake. When you're prompted to type in the text string you want to search for, type the mistake the way you made it, and the type of cells through which you want to search.

You can choose among **Formula** cells, **Label** cells, or **Both**. (You cannot search through value cells.) The next prompt lets you tell 1-2-3 whether to **Find** each cell where this string is found or **Replace** the string in each cell. Because you made a mistake and want to change the mistake, **Replace** is the choice in this instance. Tell 1-2-3 what the correct string should be and press Enter.

Each cell with that string will be highlighted in succession. You can decide whether to **Replace** the string in that cell and automatically move on to the next cell, to replace **All** of the strings everywhere at once, to skip to the **Next** cell without making a change in the current cell, or to **Quit** out of the command completely.

A Last Word on Ranges

When your data doesn't look at home on the ranges of your worksheet, 1-2-3 offers many range commands to help correct the problem. Each section of your worksheet can be tailored to your specifications, but as always, some planning and care are necessary.

Your Formulas Won't Formulate

CHAPTER THIRTEEN

Anyone who creates a Worksheet but doesn't use the power of formulas to process the data is not using 1-2-3 to its fullest potential. Anyone who does use formulas is also tapping into a wonderful new area for making mistakes.

Creating a formula is a high-level skill; but an even higher level skill is making sure that the answer is correct and will continue to be correct at printing time.

The Formula for Writing Successful Formulas

The secret to writing formulas in 1-2-3 is using cell addresses. Make the formula refer to the cell itself rather than the cell contents. If you refer to the cell and then change the contents of the cell, the formula will update automatically. However, if you refer to the contents, and then change one of the cells, the formula will remain the same.

You need to understand how formulas work in 1-2-3. When you write a formula in cell A3 that adds cells A1 and A2, you probably write +A1+A2 in cell A3. It seems sensible to think that 1-2-3 is saying to itself, "I should add the contents of cells A1 and A2." This is not what's happening, however. Instead, 1-2-3 is saying to itself, "I should add the two cells directly above the cell where I am." A *big* difference, which means that the formula can be copied to other cells and will work on the two cells directly above the cell where it is placed.

This feature is called *relative cell reference.* If a formula always referred to cells A1 and A2, then copying it around your worksheet would put the same answer (A1+A2) all over the place. But copying a formula with relative cell references means that it can be used to add cells relative to where it was copied—another reason why you should use cell addresses in formulas.

Formulas don't add labels (except in string formulas). So, if you include a cell with a label, don't worry about getting the wrong answer. Only values are acted on.

Formulas can add (+), subtract (–), multiply (*), and divide (/). If you write a formula involving more than one operation, however, it won't do them in the order they appear in the formula. For example, 3+5*2 would not return 16. Instead, a formula does multiplication, then division, then addition, and then subtraction. So, the preceding formula would return 13 because it does the 5*2 part first. To force a formula to do the addition first, include that portion in parentheses (3+5)*2.

Besides these formulas and operators, 1-2-3 offers a more advanced method of writing formulas that saves keystrokes and allows for vastly more complicated calculations. This method begins with the @ (referred to as *at*) symbol. To see a list of the @ functions, go to an empty cell and type @, and then press F1 (Help). A complete list of @ functions appears. Highlight one that interests you, and information about that one function will appear.

Fixing Your Formulas

1-2-3 formulas can sometimes be a little tricky—and a little quirky. Read ahead to discover some of the more common formula problems and how to fix them.

Problem 1:
You change the data but the answer in the formula doesn't change

Most likely, you've written the formula incorrectly. Refer to the do's and don'ts and make sure you didn't violate one of them. Remember, if you want to add the values in two cells, you should use the cell addresses in the formula rather than doing the math in your head or adding the two numbers. For example, if you enter the value 125 in cell A1 and 100 in A2, and you want to put the sum in A3, the formula you write in A3 should be +A1+A2, not 125+100.

The reason for using cell addresses is simple: If you add the numbers, the answer will always be 225; however, if you use the cell addresses, the answer changes when the cell contents change.

Ten Do's and Don'ts When Using Formulas

1. *Do* be in the cell in which you want the answer to appear.

2. *Don't* use numbers in a formula if you can avoid it. Use cell addresses instead.

3. *Do* watch out for the CIRC flag at the bottom of the screen when writing formulas.

4. *Don't* do math in your head.

5. *Do* start a formula with a plus sign (+) if it would otherwise begin with a letter.

6. *Don't* put spaces in formulas.

7. *Do* use range names in formulas instead of cell addresses if possible.

8. *Don't* write the same type of formula in many cells. Use copy instead.

9. *Do* use the F4 key to make a cell address absolute when a formula you're going to copy refers to one specific cell.

10. *Don't* forget to test the temperature of the formula with your pinky before giving it to the baby. (Gotcha!)

Problem 2:

You write a fine formula, but it returns a zero

Look at the cells you want to add. How do you do that? You go to the cell in which a value you're adding is located and look in the control panel. Make sure that the numbers there are values. Just being a number doesn't make a cell entry a value.

> **Get in Line, Please**
>
> Values are always in the right side of a cell. Yet, new users try many tricks to get values to appear in other places than the right side. These attempts will always produce undesirable results. If you succeed in realigning a value, it becomes a label and cannot be used in a formula.

Problem 3:

A formula returns a zero after /Worksheet Delete Column or Row

This situation happens when you delete data that was part of a formula. To correct the problem, immediately press Alt+F4 to undo the deletion (assuming that you have Undo enabled). If you can't do that, you'll have to insert a row and enter the lost data. The formula will also have to be edited or rewritten.

Another cause for the problem occurs when you're deleting a row or column and you delete the lower right or upper left corner of a named range. If you name a range, you can use that name in an @SUM formula.

When this problem occurs, move the cell back to its original position. To avoid this condition in the future, copy rather than move a cell's contents, and then delete the original cell's contents.

Problem 4:

You add new values at the bottom or top of a range of values, but the @SUM formula still returns the previous answer

A formula refers to a range of cells. If data is added in other cells, be sure you change the formula to include the newest cells. That change might seem obvious but it is often overlooked. This problem happens more often in an @SUM formula that refers to a named range. The named range must be expanded to include the new data or only the original data will be included in the formula. Use /**Range Name Create**, type in the name of the expanded range, and press Enter. The original range will be highlighted. Expand the highlight to cover the new data and press Enter.

Problem 5:

You wrote an @SUM formula and the answer is wrong

@SUM may not be what you wanted. The formula @SUM (A1..B4) refers to a range; contents of *all* cells between A1 and B4 are added. If only certain cells in that range should be added, you'll have to use a formula that refers to only those cells. Use +A1+A4+B4 if only those cells are to be added.

Problem 6:

You write a formula referring to one cell, copy it to other cells, and now those other cells give strange answers

The way to write a formula so that it always refers to one cell is to make the reference to that one cell absolute. Because this occurrence is common, 1-2-3 dedicated a key to the solution, the F4 (Abs) key.

Here's what to do to fix the problem. Start the formula and type +B4*B2 as before; however, before pressing Enter, press the F4 key to make the cell reference B2 absolute. The resulting cell reference looks like this: B2. The dollar sign be-

> **An Absolute Reference Is Not Always an Absolute Reference**
>
> Notice that by repeatedly pressing the F4 key, you can make only the row or only the column part of the cell reference absolute. This feature makes it possible to copy the formula to other cells while keeping either row or column reference absolute.

fore the B tells the formula always to look in column B. The dollar sign before the 2 tells it always to look in row 2. If it always looks in column B and always in row 2, it always looks in cell B2 no matter where it's copied.

Problem 7:
You copy a formula and then move it, and the results are confusing

Right. If you're not aware of the different effects Copy and Move have on formulas, you get a bit of a surprise. Just keep this in mind when deciding what to do. Moving a formula *does not* change the cell references. No matter where you move a formula, it still refers to the same cells it referred to before it was moved. But, if you copy it, the cell references change so that they're relative to the new location.

To fix the problem, decide first what you want the answer to look like after the formula is in the new place. Do you want it to refer to new cells? If so, use the Copy command to copy the formula to the new location. Do you want to have the same answer in the new cell as you have in the old one? Then, use the Move command to move the formula to the new cell.

Problem 8:
Every time you make a change anywhere in the worksheet, a formula gives a new answer

Check the bottom of the screen for the dreaded CIRC flag. Flags are little boxes at the bottom of the Worksheet that tell the status of such features as Num Lock, Caps Lock, and Undo. CIRC is a warning that something needs attention. Somewhere in your Worksheet you committed a keystroke error while writing a formula.

To find the offending formula, press /Worksheet Status. In the middle of the settings sheet is a single cell reference for a circular formula if there is one. Go to that cell and notice that the cell where the formula was written is included in the formula. Anytime you add cell entries or execute any commands, the formula recalculates, and becomes ever more inaccurate.

What's the Status?

Remember that /Worksheet Status accesses a status sheet that lists only one circular reference at a time. Check the bottom of the screen frequently to be sure no CIRC flag has appeared. If it has, go to the proper cell, edit the formula, and check again to make sure that the flag is gone. If it is not, use /Worksheet Status again, find out the next reference, fix it, and continue until the flag disappears.

After you find the cell the circular formula is in, go to that cell and press F2 (Edit) to edit the formula. The contents of the cell you're editing appear at the top of the screen. Use the left- and right-arrow keys to move around inside the formula. What you must do is delete the reference to the current cell. In other words, if the formula is in cell A3, make sure that cell A3 is not mentioned or included in the formula. Press Enter when the formula is fixed.

Problem 9:

You copy a formula too close to the edge of the worksheet and get a strange formula

Let's say you copy a formula in cell D4 to cell D1. The original formula added the two cells directly above it, D2 and D3. When that formula is copied to D1, it still looks at the two cells directly above it. What are they? As far as 1-2-3 is concerned, the adjacent row above row 1 is the bottom row, 8192. The two cells above D1, therefore, are D8192 and D8191.

Even worse is copying the same formula close to but not right to the boundary. If the formula in D4 is copied to D2, the two new cells referred to are D1 and D8192. The new formula is @SUM(D1..D8192). All cells in column D are now included, and the formula becomes circular.

Be careful when you copy cells too close to the edge of the worksheet. Awareness is your only way to deal with this strange phenomenon.

If you do make this mistake, use Undo. When you can't use Undo, you'll have to delete the formula in its new location. You may also have to reenter the data you deleted when you copied the formula to that cell.

Problem 10:

You do a file combine and formulas are now returning wrong answers

When you use /File Combine, you're asking 1-2-3 to bring all or part of another file into the current worksheet. After starting the command, you have to make a choice: Copy, Add, or Subtract. Here's where the confusion might begin. If you use /File Combine Copy to put data into the current worksheet, each cell from the incoming file replaces a cell in the target range. Cell contents of incoming cells don't change, except that formulas are brought into the new worksheet with the relative cell addresses changed. (The target range is the cells into which the new file or range will be combined. The upper left corner of the target range is wherever the cell pointer is when the command is executed.)

When /File Combine Add (or Subtract) is selected, every incoming cell is changed to a value, labels become zeros, and formulas are converted to values. These values are added to (or subtracted from) the contents of the target range. Labels and formulas in the target range are not changed, however, so these two choices don't mess up your existing formulas.

This is one of those situations where care *before* the command is important. Save your work before you do a /File Combine just to be safe. If you're confused about how the command works, start performing /File Combine; then press the F1 (Help) key and read about the meaning of the choices you must make.

Correcting a mistake made in /File Combine Copy can be difficult if Undo is not available. If you saved the current work before using /File Combine, retrieve it and start again. If it hasn't been saved, you have to reenter the lost data.

It's a bit easier to clean up after a goofed /File Combine Add or Subtract. Because your formulas weren't changed, you only need to check the target range to make sure that formulas are picking up the data in all the cells they're supposed to.

Problem 11:
You include your account number in your checkbook Worksheet

Imagine a situation in which you list a bank account number at the top of a column of figures. Then you write an @SUM formula that includes all the value cells, including the cell with the account number. It's a fine bank balance but, unfortunately, a bit inflated. There is no problem with including extra cells in an @SUM formula *if* those other cells contain labels or are empty.

Some numbers you enter into cells are really labels, ZIP codes, phone numbers, and account numbers. Unless you type a label prefix (apostrophe, quotation mark, or caret) in front of them, they'll be values. To put a label prefix in front of them, press the Edit key (F2) and notice that the cell contents are not displayed at the top of the screen. Press the Home key to move the cursor to the beginning of the cell entry and type one of the label prefixes. Apostrophes put cell contents in the left side of a cell, double quotation marks put them in the right side, and carets center them.

Problem 12:
You want a cell with a formula to stop changing when you change data

A sales manager has a worksheet that tracks sales performance for the current month. At the end of the month, the results for the month should be kept for a permanent record. The formula that has been updating itself every time data in the sheet was updated should stop updating itself. The sums for the month just ended should be kept in a different place in the worksheet, so that the worksheet is ready for data from the new month.

/Range Value to the rescue. This command allows you to cause the values that formulas are currently returning to be *frozen* and to be displayed elsewhere. Move the cell pointer to the formulas to be frozen, execute /Range Value, highlight all formulas to be frozen, and press Enter. Now move the cell pointer to a new location and press Enter. The original formula is still in place, but the value it was returning is now stored in a new place as a value, not a formula.

You could leave the cell pointer in the original cell where the formula was located. In this case, the formula is converted to a value right in the same cell.

Problem 13:
Your @AVG formula is not correct

You can highlight all the cells you want in an @SUM formula, as long as the extra cells are not values. This is not the case in @AVG. This formula sums all the cells in the range, and then divides by the number of cells. If you included some extra cells in the formula, the divisor is wrong and so is the average.

Edit the @AVG formula. Make sure that only the cells with values to be averaged are included in the formula.

A cell with a zero in it is included in the average, an empty cell is not. Therefore, don't put a zero or a label in a cell that doesn't have a value if you don't want it included in the average.

Problem 14:
You want to average only certain cells in a range of data, but all cells are averaged

Convert the @AVG to a @DAVG formula. The *D* is for Data, and the formula treats the worksheet like a database. The formula checks all numbers in the range to see whether they conform to criteria you set. If they do conform, it finds their average. Those that don't conform are ignored.

The regular @AVG formula has only a range for an argument (the information inside the parentheses). The argument for @DAVG is a bit more complicated—it includes three pieces of data. The first part of the argument is the range where the whole database is located, including the column titles. The second part is the column offset for the column being averaged. The third part is the range where the criterion is specified.

What Else Have You Got?

You also can use @DCOUNT for counting the number of filled cells that meet the criteria, @DSUM for adding specific values, @DMAX and @DMIN for finding the maximum and minimum values of conforming cells, and @DVAR and @DSTD for finding the variance or standard deviation of conforming cells.

A Final Note on Formulas

The power and complexity of formulas make them enormously useful tools, and, at the same time, offer you more opportunity to make mistakes. The more common mistakes were discussed in this chapter. The most important thing to remember about formulas is to be careful about cells to which the formulas refer. Be sure the proper cells are referred to and be careful about labels and values. Check all formula cells periodically to make sure that they're intact and working properly. As you've seen, moving, copying, file combining, and naming ranges can all have strange effects on formulas.

Your Data Won't Print Right

CHAPTER FOURTEEN

Unless you want to carry your monitor around with you so that you can show your work to people, you're going to have to print your work on paper. When user and software lock horns with hardware, the fur can fly.

For that reason, you need to understand how to get everything set up and ready to go so that when you issue the Print command, you don't get beeped.

Proper Printing Procedures

Getting your printer to work properly starts during the install routine. You're asked first whether you have a text printer and then whether you have a graphics printer. Installing a text printer allows you to use the basic 1-2-3 /**Print** command. This prints the plain worksheet.

If you want to print Wysiwyg enhancements like shading or lines or different fonts, you also must have a graphics printer installed. Otherwise, you won't have a printer to choose when you want to use the Wysiwyg **:Print** command.

In case you're wondering, you can use the same printer as both the graphics and the text printer—if your printer is that talented. And nowadays, most printers *are* that talented.

With the /**Print** menu, you have a choice of printing to a printer (the usual choice) or to a file. Printing to a file allows you to save a worksheet as a text file (ASCII) so that you can use it in virtually any program (but without formulas or Wysiwyg formatting).

In the **:Print** menu, you can choose to print to an encoded file, do background printing, or print immediately to the printer. Here is what each choice means:

- **G**o. The most common choice when someone wants to print in Wysiwyg is to choose **G**o, which sends the data to the printer. For most of the time the printer is working, you cannot use the computer. This can be a fair amount of time if a lot of data has to be printed.

Yes, the Problem Could Be in Your Hardware

Dot-matrix printers, laser printers, fonts, cartridges, cables, interfaces, and landscape and portrait print modes could be the culprits that stand between you and your printed data. Understanding how to make 1-2-3 behave is one thing, but now you have to understand how to make hardware behave, too? Yes and no. After everything is in place, your hardware worries are over, and you're back to dealing with only the software. Although dealing with hardware is not the topic of this book, it is important to be sure that the cables from computer to printer are firmly in place, that there is paper in the printer, and that the printer is turned on and is on-line.

- **B**ackground. The alternative to **Go** is **B**ackground. This choice allows you to send a job to the printer, but because the printing is going on in the background you can still use your computer for other things. If you tend to run out of memory easily, background printing may be a problem.

- **File**. The third choice in Wysiwyg printing is **File**, which creates an encoded file, one with all the Wysiwyg formatting. Later, you can print the worksheet from the DOS prompt by typing bprint followed by the name of the encoded file.

> ### Be Prepared
>
> If you intend to use background printing during a 1-2-3 session, you have to start it before you start 1-2-3; Otherwise, background printing won't work. At the DOS prompt, in the 1-2-3 directory, type bprint. Then start 1-2-3. To learn more about background printing, call up the Wysiwyg menu, select **Print**, highlight **Background**, and press F1 (Help). Alternatively, you can use **/Print Background**.

Producing the Perfect Printed Page

You can produce a polished professional document as opposed to a mediocre sheet of paper by having some knowledge of the print options and knowing how to avoid the little printing problems you might otherwise encounter.

Printing is much more than just highlighting a range of data and sending it to a piece of paper. Carefully arranging data and then using the main menu to format cells, widen columns, and align labels is a step in the right direction. Adding Wysiwyg changes makes a dull page come alive. Yet, there are still many other things you can do to make the printed page a finished and professional document.

Knowing what you can do and how to do it can be a bit confusing because 1-2-3 has two Print commands. Here is a quick overview:

- Remember that when you use the main Print menu (accessed with the slash key), you print the plain version of your worksheet without Wysiwyg enhancements. To see the Wysiwyg changes—fonts, shading, drop shadows, and lines, for example—you have to use the Wysiwyg Print command (accessed with the colon key).

What Are Headers and Footers and Why Would I Use Them?

Headers and footers are small bits of text that are automatically printed at the top or bottom of each page.

Borders are designated rows or columns which are printed on every page to prevent the reader from being confused when looking at data on pages other than the first page.

Making Choices Faster

When you invoke either Print command, a settings sheet appears and shows you what options are currently set. You have three choices for changing these settings. First, you can use the menu as you do any menu commands. The second choice is faster. After the settings sheet appears, press F2 (Edit). Notice that certain letters are highlighted in the sheet itself. By pressing the appropriate key (this is called the *hot key*), you can enter the individual sections of the settings sheet and make changes directly to that section by using the keyboard. Faster yet is the third method: using the mouse. Put the mouse pointer (the arrow) on the item you want to change; then click on the choice or type the setting you want.

- Just because you're using the main Print menu, however, doesn't mean you can't tailor the printout to your specifications. In the options part of this menu are commands to add headers and footers, change the margins, place borders on each page, and change the number of lines you print on a page.

- The Wysiwyg Print menu allows even more changes. In the Settings menu, you can choose to add a grid or worksheet frame to the worksheet or change the page number printed on each page. With the Layout menu, you can change the page size, add headers and footers (different from the header or footer set in the main menu), change margins, and add borders.

10 Do's and Don'ts for Printing

1. *Do* use compression in the Wysiwyg menu to fit the range to the page.

2. *Don't* include borders in the print range.

3. *Don't* assume the default page length of 66 lines in the /**P**rint menu will be correct on all printers.

4. *Do* use setup strings in the main menu to change printer settings, such as compressed settings.

5. *Don't* forget that margins in the main Print menu are measured in characters. In the Wysiwyg menu, they are measured in inches or millimeters.

6. *Do* highlight as far to the right as necessary to include all text in the print range.

7. *Don't* forget to hide columns you don't want printed.

8. *Do* remember that landscape printing means sideways printing, not printing country scenes. Dot-matrix printers can do landscape printing only in Release 2.4, not in Release 2.3.

9. *Do* be sure that you've properly installed a text and a graphics printer during install.

10. *Don't* get mad if you have to wait more than two or three seconds for the printer to print. Sometimes a print job can take a long time.

Dealing with Print Problems

Even after you've taken all precautions with your hardware and the print commands, you can still expect to encounter some problems from time to time. Here is what to do to avoid or deal with them.

Problem 1:

You issued one of the print commands and the printer doesn't start

Be sure the printer is plugged in and turned on and that all cables are in firmly. Check to be sure the printer has paper and is on-line. Also, be sure that you've selected the correct printer. For printing from the main menu, select the printer by selecting /Worksheet Global Default Printer Name. In the Wysiwyg menu, you choose :Print Config Printer. Finally, be sure to select the right interface. Use /Worksheet Global Default Interface for the main menu or :Print Config Interface for Wysiwyg printing.

Network Tangles

Printing on a network means you must designate a logical port as the interface. Choose LPT1, LPT2, or LPT3 as the interface. Also choose the proper network printer, not the local printer.

Problem 2:

When you use /Print, gaps appear in the middle of a page

When you're printing from the main menu, select Align from the Print menu before printing. This tells the printer that it is to start printing at the top of the page. Otherwise, the printer may decide to start somewhere down the page and put page breaks (the gaps) somewhere in the middle of the page.

Problem 3:
When you use /Print, the page break occurs sooner on each successive page

Some printers expect a different page length than the default 66 lines per page. Set the correct page length with /**W**orksheet **G**lobal **D**efault **P**rinter **P**age-Length.

When Length Really Does Matter

Here's a trick to determine the page length for your printer: Do a /**D**ata **F**ill in the first hundred cells in column A (from 1 to 100). Now print that column using the /Print command. The last number printed on the first page is the page length.

Problem 4:
You're printing to different size paper than the usual 8 1/2 by 11

From the main menu, set page length as just described. From the Wysiwyg menu, use **:P**rint **L**ayout **P**age-Size and choose the proper size. If none of the selections

---
English or Metric?

Setting custom page sizes from either the main menu or the Wysiwyg menu is easy. Type the measurement, a space, and then *in* for inches, *mm* for millimeters, and *cm* for centimeters. (Wysiwyg converts centimeters to millimeters.) Another way to set custom page sizes is to use the F2 (Edit) key to edit the settings sheet. After pressing F2, press *U* for units, *I* for inches, or *M* for millimeters. Yet another way is to use the mouse to click on the proper choice.

---

match the paper you're using, select **C**ustom from the menu and type the length and width of the sheets.

Problem 5:
On your printout, page breaks occur in the wrong place

Several solutions can help you with this problem. From the main menu, you can place a page break in the row you want by putting the cell pointer in the proper row and selecting /**W**orksheet **P**age.

This inserts a blank row and puts a double colon (::) in the row to show the page break. If you decide to delete this row later, be careful; you may have placed data in that row.

In Wysiwyg, you can put a page break in a column or a row by selecting **:Worksheet Page Column** or **Row**.

Hold on There!

Before putting in page breaks, you might want to try **:Print Layout Compression Automatic**. This command reduces the size of the print range so that it might fit on one page. If it doesn't, you can use **:Print Layout Compression Manual** and enter your own guess as to how much to compress the range to make it fit. Be careful not to shrink it so much that only a mosquito can read it.

Problem 6:

You know you have more fonts on your laser printer, but they don't appear on your printouts

If the fonts you want to use are on a font cartridge, you must select this cartridge in the Wysiwyg menu. Use **:Print Config** and **1st-Cart** or **2nd-Cart** and type the name of the cartridge.

Printing A-Go-Go

A client once called our office and complained that every time she tried to print, 1-2-3 printed the same worksheet three times on the paper. After lots of questioning, we figured out the problem: She was impatient. When she used the Print command, she pressed G for Go, but nothing happened. So she pressed G again. Still nothing. So she pressed it a third time. Three's a charm, and on the third G, the printer started—so she assumed that pressing G three times was necessary. (It isn't.) It just took a while for the first G to take effect, and then the other two were executed in their turn. The result? Three copies. The moral? Be patient, and give the printer a chance.

Problem 7:

You hate waiting for the printer to finish printing so that you can get back to work

The background Print command in Wysiwyg allows you to print and work at the same time. If you plan to use this option, you must type bprint at the DOS prompt in the 1-2-3 program directory before starting 1-2-3. When the time comes to print, select **:Print Background**, or **/Print Background**. You can then go on working while the printer is printing.

Problem 8:

Wysiwyg enhancements don't print

If you want the fonts, shading, lines, and other fancy Wysiwyg additions to your worksheet, you must use the Wysiwyg **:Print** command. The main **/Print** command prints the worksheet with no Wysiwyg formatting.

> **Nothing Fancy, Please**
>
> To see your worksheet completely free of every 1-2-3 option, use the main print menu and choose **/Print Printer Options Other Cell-Formulas**. Choosing Cell Formulas prints formulas rather than the answers in the cells in which you placed formulas. Choosing Unformatted prints your work without headers, footers, or hard page breaks.

Problem 9:

You want to print several sections of the worksheet on one sheet

From the main **Print** menu, highlight one print range and print it, and then highlight another section. Before choosing **G**o, don't choose **Align**. Not choosing **Align** causes 1-2-3 to continue printing on the same page. 1-2-3 does not add the header, page numbers, or other beginning-of-page formats.

To do this in Wysiwyg, you have to copy the various sections to one location and then include them all in one print range. At the end of a Wysiwyg **Print** command, the paper is advanced to the next page.

Problem 10:

The same print range is highlighted every time you try to print

The **Print** command is sticky. This means that it remembers the print range from the last time you printed. If you

> **Or Better Yet...**
>
> Highlight the print range before you start to print. Use the mouse to highlight the range or press F4 (Abs) and then highlight the range you want to print. After that, call up either **Print** menu and the range is already set for you.

want to print a different range, highlighting the old range can be a pain. You can find an easy way around this, though—especially if your cell pointer is positioned in a corner of the new print range. When the old range is highlighted, press Backspace. This removes the highlight from the old range and returns the cell pointer to the original cell. Now simply anchor the cell pointer and highlight the new range.

Problem 11:
When you choose Go from the Wysiwyg print menu, you get an Out of Memory error

If Wysiwyg printing causes you to run out of memory, you'll have to reduce memory usage. See Chapter 4, "Dealing with Disaster When It Strikes," for a list of steps you can take to free up some memory. The quickest way is to turn the Undo feature off temporarily by using /Worksheet Global Default Other Undo Disable.

Problem 12:
You want to print a selected group of pages rather than the entire print range

Use the Wysiwyg menu and choose :Settings and then Begin and End to designate the first and last pages to be printed. In the main /Print menu, you must reduce the print range to only the data you want printed.

Problem 13:
You need to stop printing after one page so that you can feed another sheet into the printer

Again use the Wysiwyg menu. Choose :Print Settings Wait Yes. After a page is printed, the printer waits until you manually feed the next sheet and choose **G**o before it prints the next page. Don't forget to set **W**ait **N**o from the same menu if you want to return to continuous printing later.

Problem 14:
You highlighted all the cells where you placed data, but not all the data appeared on the printout

Highlighting the cells where you entered the data is not enough. You must highlight far enough to the right to be sure the data that spills out of the cells is included in the total range. Otherwise, your data will be truncated in the printout.

Problem 15:
You're trying to highlight a print range, but you can only see one corner at a time

When you highlight a large print range, you can see only one part of the range at a time. When you want to make sure that you high-lighted all the data you want to print, seeing it all can be a problem.

Remember that you can press the period key while you're highlighting a range. Each time you do this, you move the cell pointer clockwise to the next corner. Not only can

> ### What's in the Range?
>
> Sometimes a range is so big that it is not possible to see all edges of it. How can you tell whether all the data you want is included? Set the Wysiwyg print range and then exit the Print menu. The dotted line of the print range remains on the screen so that you can check all edges of the range and be sure everything is included. When you're sure all the necessary data is there, print.

you see a different corner of the print range, but you can also high-light outward from that corner.

Problem 16:

You don't like where 1-2-3 puts the page breaks

Page breaks can be added with the main menu or the Wysiwyg menu. The main menu, however, can only put page breaks in rows, so you can't use this menu to force a column's data to be printed on a particular page. Move to the row where you want the page break and execute /Worksheet Page. A row is inserted and a page break symbol (::) is added.

To use the Wysiwyg menu, move to the row or column where you want a page break and choose :Worksheet Page, then Column or Row and press Enter. The dotted lines you see are the page breaks.

Problem 17:

You want all data to appear on one page but instead it is printed on several pages

The Wysiwyg menu includes a menu item for fitting your print range to a single page. Naturally, you can't expect to fit 4000 cells on one page, but within reason the :Print Layout Compression command will do the trick. In most cases, use :Print Layout Compression Automatic. If the automatic option doesn't give you the results you like, choose Manual and Enter the amount of compression you want. Remember that both the length and width are adjusted to fit the page. Experiment with different amounts of compression. Use :Print Preview to be sure the pages look the way you want them to.

What Does It Say?

If you set the compression too high, the printed characters will be so small you can't read them. Rather than waste paper experimenting, use :Print Preview to check the proposed printout. If it is hard to see the text, press F6 (Window) and then + to enlarge the display. Pressing – (minus) shrinks the display, and pressing * returns to the default display. Use the arrow keys to move the display around when it is enlarged.

You can set the compression to less than 100 percent in order to make a small range fill more of the printed page.

Using the main Print menu, you can also instruct the printer to use compressed print, which produces smaller letters and allows more data to be printed on a page. Use /Print Printer Options Setup; then type \ and your printer's code for compressed printing. These codes are listed in your printer manual. For example, the setup string for compressed printing on an Epson printer is \015. The subject of printer control codes is covered in detail in Que's *Using 1-2-3* books.

Problem 18:

You printed a report that took several sheets of paper. After page 1, you can't tell which column or row the data is in.

Chances are, you typed the title of each column at the top of the column. You also may have typed a row title at the left side of each row. You can ask 1-2-3 to print those title columns or rows (or both) on every page so you won't have to guess at what goes where on succeeding pages. Columns or rows with titles printed on every page are called *borders*.

Because the borders feature is so useful, it appears in both the main Print menu and the Wysiwyg Print menu. In either case, start with your cell pointer in a row or column where you're going to make a border. Then use either /Worksheet Print Printer Options Borders Rows (or Columns) or :Print Layout Borders Top (or Left). If necessary, you can anchor the cell pointer (use the period key) in the row or column and highlight others to be part of the border.

Problem 19:

You designated borders and now they appear twice in the printout

The solution here is not to include the border rows in the print range. Because they are borders, they will print anyway, and if they are included in the print range, they will print again.

Problem 20:

You want to highlight a large print range, but pressing the down-arrow key 200 times doesn't appeal to you

You can use most of the cursor-movement keys in addition to the arrow keys for highlighting ranges. PgDn and Tab are good for moving long distances, but the GoTo key (F5) does not work.

Here is the best way to highlight all your data when it covers a very large range: When you're highlighting the print range, anchor the cell pointer and then press End followed by Home. This extends your highlight to the lower right corner of the active area of the worksheet. The entire data area is highlighted.

> **Where Am I??**
>
> You might press End Home to get to the lower right corner of your data but wind up further down or to the right more than you wanted. This happened because you used a cell or formatted a range way out there. Now 1-2-3 thinks that's part of your worksheet. Delete all unnecessary data beyond the useful data, unformat (and unprotect) all those cells beyond the data. Now, after you save and retrieve the file, the active area will be a bit more manageable.

Problem 21:

Your data doesn't fill the sheet to the bottom, but it's so wide it takes two sheets

Consider using landscape printing. Landscape prints sideways, so the top of your data is printed along the long side of the paper. Use the Wsyiwyg Print menu and select :Print Config Orientation Landscape. Remember that this works only on dot-matrix printers and only in Release 2.4.

Problem 22:

You use headers and footers, but they are always printed on the left side of the paper

On your keyboard is a key with a symbol called the *pipe* symbol, which usually appears as a broken vertical line (¦). You use this symbol to place headers and footers.

Text entered without a pipe symbol is printed at the left margin. Any text with one pipe symbol in front of it is centered, and any text with two pipe symbols in front of it is aligned with the right margin. This means that

> | |Top Secret

prints the words Top Secret at the right margin.

How about a Date?

You might want the current date to appear in a header or footer. The @ symbol accomplishes that. For page numbers, use the # symbol. A header with

> Your Department|@|Page #

prints Your Department at the left margin, the current date in the center, and Page with the correct page number at the right margin.

The pipe symbols also work when you separate them. For example, you could type the following header:

> Your Name|Your Department|Report Title

Your Name would print at the left margin, Your Department would be centered, and Report Title would print at the right margin.

Problem 23:

You want a header or footer to be the same text as a certain cell. You're afraid that you might change the cell but forget to change the header or footer.

After issuing the commands to write a header, type the address of the cell you want to be the header. Just remember to type \ first. This means that if you want the contents of cell A1 to be a header, type \a1 when prompted to enter the header or footer text. Change A1 all you want, and when the time comes to print, the current contents of that cell will be the header (or footer). The only drawback is that the text will be printed at the left margin.

Problem 24:
Wysiwyg enhancements look good on-screen, but not so good on the printout

The solution here comes before you print. You can take two steps to be sure the Wysiwyg enhancements that look so nice on the screen will not mess up your printout. First, if you're using a black-and-white printer, switch your display to black and white by using **:Display Mode B&W**. Now your display looks a lot more like the printout. While in this display mode, use **:Print Preview** to see what the final product will look like. Be sure to check cells where you used colors or shading. Sometimes these settings interfere with the text when everything is black, white, and gray.

If things don't look good in the preview, go to the necessary cells and change the Wysiwyg enhancements. Be sure you see a big contrast between background and text.

A Last Printed Word on Printing

Sometimes your work is going to be seen only on the screen, and other times, your work will be seen primarily in printed form. As you arrange data and add Wysiwyg changes, keep in mind the form the final product will take. What looks good on-screen may not look so good on paper.

Without the print commands, 1-2-3 would be much less useful. But, without the frustrations of dealing with options and cables and plugs, life would be a bit easier. You'll find that the print commands are manageable, once you learn where all the features are located within the menus.

Finally, be sure you know the differences between the main and the Wysiwyg **P**rint menus. What you choose in one menu has no effect on the other menu.

What To Do When...

Your Formatting Is Wrong

CHAPTER FIFTEEN

Sometimes, values or cells don't look quite the way you want them to. When this happens, you need to use a format command. As always, there are a few things that can go wrong, and this chapter helps you figure out how to make formatting commands work the way you want them to.

What Is Formatting?

There are two ways to access formatting commands: on the 1-2-3 main menu using the / or on the Wysiwyg menu using the :. If you use the 1-2-3 main menu, you have the following two choices for formatting:

- /Worksheet **Global Format** sets the appearance for all numbers in the entire worksheet.

- /Range **Format** sets the appearance of values on specific cells or ranges that you highlight and takes precedence over the /Worksheet **Global Format** command.

The main menu commands only change the way a value is displayed. The value itself doesn't change—regardless of the format you pick—only its appearance changes. Remember: this command only works on values.

If you go to a single cell and use the /Range **Format** command to change the value so it looks like a percent, you can then use the /Worksheet **Global Format** command to change the appearance of all values in the worksheet to currency. The single cell formatted as a percent, however, does not change. /Range **Format** takes precedence over /Worksheet **Global Format** whether you use it before or after the /Work-sheet **Global Format** command.

Well, Almost...

There is one main menu formatting command that you can use to change the appearance of labels—/Range **Format Hidden**. The contents of any cell formatted with the **Hidden** command disappear from view. You can use the **Hidden** command to conceal privileged information or to make your spreadsheet look neater by hiding less important material.

To change the appearance of a cell or the appearance of a cell's contents, you can use the Wysiwyg formatting command, :**Format**. When you format using this method, it doesn't matter whether the cell contains values or labels.

Here are some of the changes you can make to a cell or a range using the Wysiwyg :**Format** command:

- Change the font

- Make the cell contents bold

- Italicize the cell contents

- Underline the cell contents

- Change colors for the background and the text

- Add lines to the sides of the cell or range

- Add a drop shadow

- Add shading

A slightly faster way to use either the main menu /**R**ange **F**ormat command or the Wysiwyg **:F**ormat command is to highlight the range first, and then access the proper menu and execute the com-mand. This method is called *range preselection*, and you can use either the keyboard or the mouse to select the range.

To preselect a range with the mouse, place the mouse cursor in a corner of the range you want to

---

Can You? Icon

Sorry about that. In Release 2.4, the icons visible along the right side of the screen enable you to do certain commands more quickly. For instance, the box containing the *B* allows you to make a cell or range bold; the *I* allows you to italicize; and the *$* lets you format values as currency with two decimal places.

---

format. Press and hold the left mouse button, and drag the mouse cursor to the opposite corner of the range you are formatting. Release the mouse, access the proper menu, and execute the command.

To preselect a range with the keyboard, place the cell pointer in a corner of the range you are formatting. Press the F4 (Abs) key, and then use the arrow keys to extend the highlight to all the other cells you want to format. Finally, access the appropriate menu and format command.

Preselecting a range is a faster method because it enables you to perform several commands on the same range without having to highlight the range over and over. Preselect a range, then use as many main menu and Wysiwyg format commands as you like. Then, when you're completely finished formatting, press Esc to unselect the range.

Similar to the format commands are those commands in the main menu that change the alignment of labels. They are similar because they help a spreadsheet look better by changing the way data is displayed in cells. However, this is not formatting. It is label alignment and has nothing to do

But, on the Other Hand...

You can also align labels as you type them. Type a double quotation mark (") before a label, and it will align on the right side of the cell. Type a caret (^) before the label and it will be centered in the cell. And, finally, type an apostrophe before a label and it will align on the left side of the cell. A faster method of alignment, however, is to use the /Range Label or /Worksheet Global Label-Prefix command, because you can align many labels at once.

with the format commands. As with so many other commands, /Worksheet Global Label-Prefix allows you to determine how all labels will be aligned in all cells. To change the way an individual label or a group of labels is aligned, use /Range Label, and then choose Left, Right, or Center.

10 Do's and Don'ts When Formatting Your Data

1. *Do* consider preselecting the range before you start executing the commands.

2. *Don't* use /Worksheet Global Format if you are only intending to format a few numbers.

3. *Do* keep the number of different fonts and other Wysiwyg formats to a manageable minimum. Too much variety is confusing and makes your spreadsheet difficult to read.

4. *Don't* try to use /Range Format on labels; it won't harm them, but it won't change them either.

5. *Do* enter dates as values if you need to use those dates in calculations. See Problem 8 for more information.

6. *Don't* try to realign values in cells. They always will be aligned on the right side of the cell.

7. *Do* use the align commands rather than label prefixes to align commands. It's a lot faster.

8. *Don't* try to put a drop shadow around a range that is inside a range that has its own drop shadow, or that overlaps a range with a shadow. This either won't work or it will look funny.

9. *Do* use :Format Reset to remove, all at once, all Wysiwyg formats from a cell or range, instead of removing them individually.

10. *Don't* use /Worksheet Global Format Hidden unless you want all your data to disappear. Be careful.

After committing to memory all these do's and don'ts, you still may encounter an occasional formatting problem with some of the data you enter in your spreadsheet. Read on to discover what some of these problems may be and what you can do about them.

Problem 1:
Every time you enter a value it has the wrong format, no matter where you enter it

You probably used /Worksheet Global Format to change the appearance of one or two numbers. What you've forgotten is that every cell is now formatted with that same format. Use /Range Format to change just a few numbers.

If you run into this problem, use /Worksheet Global Format General to return the default format to no format at all.

Problem 2:
In some places when you enter values, you get one format; in other places you get another format

There are a couple of mistakes you could have made here. First, as in Problem 1, you may have used the /Worksheet Global command to format just a few numbers, which changed the default format everywhere. The second possibility is that you used the /Range Format command on more cells than you really intended to format.

You can see if a cell has a unique range format by placing the cell pointer in that cell and then looking in the control panel. Any range formats you have set are displayed following the cell address. For instance, if you formatted cell A1 with currency, two decimal places, the control panel would display the following:

    A1: (C2)

The C2 represents currency, two decimal places. Remember, the control panel only shows you range formats—not global formats.

To remove a range format, use /Range Format Reset. This command returns the highlighted cells to whatever was set as the global format. They no longer have their own unique format.

Problem 3:
Now and then, you enter a value that doesn't get any format at all

You may have accidentally turned the value into a label. How did you do it? If you press the space bar before you start typing the number, or if you type one of the three label prefixes before you type the number, you'll turn the value into a label. Labels cannot be formatted. Reenter the number without spaces or a label prefix.

Problem 4:
You typed a value with a label prefix and a dollar sign. Now a formula that uses that number returns zero.

The label prefix turns a value into a label. The numerical value of a label is zero, so the number you typed has no numerical value. It looks like a number to you, but to 1-2-3 it might as well say *rutabaga*. Remember, you can't realign a value, and you must use the format commands to add the dollar sign and decimal places to a number.

The solution to this problem is to reenter the number; but this time, type only the number and then format it.

Problem 5:

You deleted a value from a cell and typed in a new value, but the new value has the same format as the old number

Right. Deleting a cell does not delete the format. If you want a new format, you have to use /Range Format to change it.

Problem 6:

You entered a number in a range and formatted it for percent. After formatting, the number expressed as a percent was too large.

Trying to format a cell with the number 50 is not the same as formatting a cell with the number .5. The second number, .5, is the same as 1/2 or 50%. Enter .5 into a cell and use /Range Format Percent 2 (for two decimal places) and you'll get 50%. Enter 50 into a cell and use the same command, and you'll get 5000.00%. The easiest way to enter a percent is to type the number followed by the percent sign. This is the only time you can type a symbol as you enter a number.

Problem 7:

OK. You typed 50 and a percent sign just like we told you and got 0.5. That doesn't look like 50%.

That's true. But if the cell isn't formatted for percent with two decimal places, your value won't have that format. 1-2-3 enters all numbers without format.

Format the cell with percent, two decimal places, and it will look the way it should.

So why type the number with the percent sign? Because many people have trouble remembering what decimal becomes what percent. So type the percent the way you want to see it. Even though 1-2-3 converts it to a decimal, you can use formatting to display it as a percent.

Problem 8:

You want to do date math, but you've been entering dates as labels

Sometimes, it's necessary to do math with dates. For example, you might have to calculate for depreciation how long your company has owned a piece of equipment. Or, you might want to calculate how long an employee has worked for the company, or figure out how many days until your next birthday, or how many days old you are (be prepared for a shock).

To enter a date as a value use the @DATE function. Type:

> @DATE(

After the opening parenthesis type a two-digit number representing the year (three digits starting with 100 for the 21st century). For example, you would type 93 for 1993. Next, type a comma and a two-digit number representing the month, for instance 03 for March. Finish the command with a comma, a two-digit number representing the day, and a closing parenthesis.

Feeling Brave and Curious?

To calculate how many days old you are, move to an empty cell and type:

> @TODAY–@date()

Inside the parentheses, type the numbers representing the date you were born (for example, (54,03,31) for March 31, 1954). Press Enter and go take some vitamins.

To enter May 28, 1979 as a value, you would type:

> @DATE(79,05,28)

Problem 9:

You entered a date and got a strange number

That number represents the number of days that have elapsed since January 1, 1900. Every day since then has its own number in 1-2-3, and that is how date math is done. Of course, unless you want your dates to look like something from Star Trek, you have to format them to look like dates. Use /Range Format Date and highlight each choice until you find the date format you prefer; then press Enter.

Problem 10:
You picked a date format, pressed Enter, and got stars

Some date formats use more characters than the default width of the column. Use :Worksheet Column Set-Width to widen the column. After you do that, the stars should not be out tonight.

Problem 11:
You made a number bold and got stars

Same as in Problem 10. The bold format makes a value take up more space in a cell, so sometimes using bold makes a value change to stars. As in Problem 10, widen the column.

Problem 12:
You entered a formula and formatted it, now you see the formula instead of the answer

You mistakenly used /Range Format Text. This format displays the actual formula rather than its answer. Change to another format and the problem should be corrected.

The +/– format displays numbers as a series of plus or minus signs. The number *3* would look like +++ if you formatted its cell with the +/– format. The number *–2* would look like - - if you used the +/– format. The number *1000* would return stars because you can't fit 1000 plus signs in a single cell.

A Last Word on Formatting

You can use formatting commands to make a plain and confusing spreadsheet look more appealing and much easier to read. Combine the correct display of values with a few Wysiwyg formats, and you have a quality presentation.

Several other chapters in this book can help you with formatting. Chapter 7 helps you with the display of your spreadsheet, Chapter 9 suggests some solutions when you have problems entering data, and, finally, Chapter 12 provides information to help you improve the appearance of ranges.

What To Do When. . .

Your Files Are Funky

CHAPTER SIXTEEN

When it's on the screen, it's a worksheet; but when it's saved to disk, it becomes a file. If it is on the screen and you turn your computer off or exit 1-2-3, does your worksheet become a file or a mere memory?

Do you have good file maintenance habits? Do you know how to avoid mistakes in dealing with files in 1-2-3? Knowing how to protect your work from permanent loss is the most important computing knowledge you can have.

Save Me!

The concept of memory in computers is confusing to some users. Simply stated, there are two main kinds of memory: temporary and permanent. The temporary memory is known as *RAM* (random-access memory). When your computer is on, the RAM is active, keeping track of programs you're using, dealing with activities going on in the background, and remembering the data you're entering into your worksheet. When you turn your computer off, the RAM is immediately emptied. That's why it is called *temporary* storage.

You have to take steps to save your worksheet to a permanent storage medium before you exit 1-2-3; otherwise, all your work goes to data heaven and is lost forever. There is no getting it back. Unfortunately, exiting the program without saving your work is one of those Oops! that can't be solved with the Undo feature.

Permanent storage usually means disks (although there are other kinds of permanent storage media like tapes and CDs). You'll find two kinds of disks. The hard disk is permanently mounted inside your computer and is able to store a lot of data. Floppy disks are the kind you can remove from your disk drive and use in another computer or store in a safe place.

The Who, Where, When, Why, and How of File Maintenance

This sounds like a primer on writing a newspaper article, doesn't it? These items represent the basics you should know about saving and working with your 1-2-3 data files.

Who?

You need to save and back up your data files. No one is going to do it for you. There is no company employee who barges into each office from time to time to save to disk the work that is being entered into each computer. If you put off saving your file—trying to do just a *little* more data entry before you save—and there's a power failure or other catastrophe (see Chapter 4), all your recent work is lost.

Where?

Using DOS, you should create a directory on your hard disk that is used exclusively for the storage of the data you create. Whether you have separate directories for worksheets and word processing documents is unimportant. What is important is that you have in its own directory the data you create.

One major reason for this suggestion is that you can see the files easier if they are not mixed up with a lot of program files. Hundreds of files may be stored in program directories. When you try to list, back up, delete, or copy your data files, the program files get in the way and may be accidentally copied, deleted, or backed up with the data.

When?

How often you take that valuable second or two to save your work depends on your working speed and your sense of adventure. If you're a hunt-and-peck typist and do five keystrokes a minute, frequent saving might be a waste of time. On the other hand, after you've entered a big chunk of data into a worksheet, the time to save has surely arrived.

If you're a gambler and prefer to assume that nothing bad will happen to you or your computer until the data on the screen is complete and perfect, wait until you're done to save.

Why?

Obviously, data is extremely vulnerable until it is saved to disk. If you haven't gotten that message yet, put this book down and take up a less challenging line of work like sorting laundry.

How?

First, create the separate directory before you start 1-2-3. After starting 1-2-3, tell it that you want to save your work to the directory you've created. Choose /Worksheet Global Default Directory and type the drive and directory name. To make this change permanent, use /Worksheet Global Default Update.

To make a temporary change in the disk or directory you're using, choose /File Directory and type the disk or directory you want to use for a while. This selection is active until you quit 1-2-3 or until you change it with either of the two commands just mentioned.

To save a file for the first time, use /File Save. Because this is the first time you saved the file, you need to name it. Any name of up to eight characters (no spaces) will do. Think of a name that later will help you identify the type of data in the file.

From now on, when you save your work, use /File Save. The program remembers the name you used before and plans to use that name again. Press Enter to accept that name.

Whenever 1-2-3 saves a file under an existing name, it prompts you with a Cancel Replace Backup option, just in case you don't want to save the updated file with the file name you used before. Cancel stops the whole save operation. Replace replaces the older version of the worksheet on disk with the updated worksheet on-screen under the existing file name. Backup renames the older version using the same file name but with a .BAK extension and saves the newest version under the file name with a .WK1 extension.

10 Do's and Don'ts for Managing Files in 1-2-3

1. *Do* save your work shortly after you start it and save it often.

2. *Don't* save your data to the directory where the program files are stored.

3. *Do* keep floppy disk backups of all your data.

4. *Don't* forget to follow DOS naming conventions in naming your file. Use up to eight characters and use no spaces in your file names.

5. *Do* save a worksheet before retrieving another.

6. *Don't* use /File Erase carelessly. Remember that /File Erase removes a file permanently from disk.

7. *Do* consider using the Backup option when saving work.

8. *Don't* expect to use Undo to correct file saving mistakes.

9. *Do* remember that the cell pointer position is saved with the file. Put it where you want it to be when you retrieve the file.

10. *Don't* expect to retrieve .WK3 worksheets into 2.X versions of 1-2-3.

Speaking of extensions, .WK1 identifies a file as one created and saved in one of the 2.X releases of 1-2-3 (2.01, 2.2, 2.3, or 2.4). A file saved in one of the 3.X versions of 1-2-3 uses the .WK3 extension. You cannot retrieve .WK3 files into a 2.X release. You can, however, retrieve a .WK1 file into a 3.X release.

Enhancement features added in a later release may be shaved off when the worksheet is retrieved into an earlier version. Some macro commands and the Wysiwyg features are good examples of this.

Fixing Your File Problems

Knowing how to deal with some of the potential file problems will make managing your files much more successful and, hopefully, will keep some of the wolves from your door. Read on to learn more about these problems.

Problem 1:
You try to save or retrieve a file but 1-2-3 keeps looking in the wrong place

When you save or retrieve a file, 1-2-3 has to look for the file somewhere. The program has to pick a disk and a directory on that disk. By default, 1-2-3 retrieves from and saves to the program directory, the place on your disk where the program files are stored.

Creating and using a separate directory for your working files is a better alternative for many reasons. (One reason is that it is much easier to back up your data files if they are in their own directory.)

To change the default directory, use /Worksheet Global Default Directory. At the prompt, press Esc to clear the original directory, and then type the name of the disk drive and directory (the path) where files should be saved from now on. (Be sure the directory has already been created before you type in its name.) Problem 2 explains how to make the change permanent across work sessions.

Problem 2:

The change to a different directory you made with /Worksheet Global Default Directory doesn't last into the next session

This happens because you didn't make the changes permanent. Executing this command changes defaults, for sure, but unless you also select Update, the changes are forgotten when you exit 1-2-3. When you start a new session, the old defaults return if you didn't choose Update. This command actually updates a file in the 1-2-3 program so that the changes are permanent.

Problem 3:

You want to save to and retrieve from another directory or disk for this session only, but 1-2-3 keeps looking in the default directory

Use /**File Directory** to change the save/retrieve directory temporarily. The next time you start 1-2-3, the original default directory will again be the one used.

If you want to save just one file to a different place—for example, when you want to save a file to a floppy in drive A—use /**File Save**. An Enter Name of file to save: prompt appears with the default drive and directory displayed after the colon. Press Esc until there is nothing after the colon. Now type the path and the file name under which the file is to be saved. (The *path* is the drive and the directory where you want to save the file.) For instance, to save a file called *salesrpt* to drive A, type **a:salesrpt** and press Enter.

Problem 4:

You don't see the file you want to retrieve during file retrieve

There are three possible reasons for this. One is that you can see only five file names at a time. To see the whole list of available files, press F3 (Names). This temporarily puts your worksheet out of view and allows you to see the whole list of files in the default directory.

The second reason is that the file doesn't exist (or you're looking for the wrong file name). The Viewer add-in can help you look at the contents of each file on the disk to see whether the data you want is under a different file name.

The third reason is that 1-2-3 may be looking in the wrong directory. You can change the default directory as mentioned previously or press Esc until the prompt says Enter Name of file to retrieve: with nothing displayed after the colon. Now type the name of the directory or disk where you think the file is and press Enter. If you don't know in which directory the file is stored, the Viewer add-in is especially useful.

Let Me in!

The only way to retrieve a 3.X file in a 2.X release is to save the file again in 3.X. This time, before you save, display the /Worksheet Global Default Ext Save menu and choose WK1 as the format for saving. Now save the file in 3.X, and it will be retrievable in 2.X. Even though it will be retrievable in 2.x, none of the special 3.x functions will be transferred. An even easier method is to type the full name using the .WK1 extension.

Problem 5:
You get an error message when attempting to retrieve a .WK3 file in a 2.X release of 1-2-3

The 3.X releases of 1-2-3 are significantly different from the 2.X releases and, therefore, worksheets created in 3.X cannot be retrieved.

Problem 6:
Every time you retrieve a file, a macro executes

You may write a macro that executes automatically every time you retrieve a file. If you don't want this to happen, select /Worksheet

Global Default Autoexec No. Now the autoexec macro will not execute. But don't forget to issue the command that makes sure these macros will execute in the future—that command is /Worksheet Global Default Autoexec Yes.

> ### On Autopilot
>
> You may be wondering how to write an autoexec macro, one that executes every time a file is retrieved. Write the macro and then name it \0 (that is, backslash zero). A macro so named is a special one that is automatically invoked one time during file retrieval. An example might be a macro that executes /File Retrieve and pauses so you can highlight the file you want to retrieve.

Problem 7:

You want 1-2-3 to retrieve a file automatically every time you start the program instead of retrieving it yourself

A file named AUTO123 will fit into your plan rather nicely. Be sure the file is in the default directory and then start 1-2-3. The file will be automatically retrieved.

Problem 8:

You retrieve a file and the worksheet on-screen disappears

Yup. That's the way it works. Be sure to save the current worksheet before retrieving another. Retrieving a new file removes whatever is on the screen. Of course, if Undo is enabled, you can press Alt+F4 to undo the retrieval. If Undo is not on,

> ### Don't Shoot First and Ask Questions Later
>
> If the following prompt appears when you start to retrieve a file, heed it!
>
> ```
> No Yes
> WORKSHEET CHANGES NOT SAVED!
>     Retrieve file anyway?
> ```
>
> The No is highlighted, but you'd be amazed how many people highlight Yes and press Enter, and then wonder where the data went. Don't be too quick to answer Yes to a prompt. 1-2-3 is trying to tell you to consider saving your data first.

the data entered since the last save is lost and gone forever.

Problem 9:

You want to combine the data from another file into the current worksheet, but /File Retrieve deletes the current file from the screen

---
A Handy Add-In

Among the add-ins available in 1-2-3 is one called Viewer. Once attached with /Addin Attach, Viewer allows you to see into files on disk, highlight the range or the file you want, and link data into the active sheet. Be sure the cell pointer is in the upper left corner of the target range before you invoke Viewer.

Use /**File Combine**. This command brings with it several decisions: Do you want part of the file or the whole file? Do you want to copy the data into the worksheet? (All data in the target range will be replaced.) Would you prefer to add or subtract the incoming data from data in the target range? See Chapter 7 for more information about /**File Combine**.

Problem 10:

You use /File Combine over valuable data.

Use Undo. Failing that, you'll have to retrieve the file and hope you saved it recently. This is one of those situations when it's important to proceed with care before issuing the command. Be sure the cell pointer is in the proper place before you start the command.

Problem 11:

You want to have a template of a file on disk that you can retrieve every so often and fill in, but when you save it, the template is lost

Creating a template means having a blank form on disk that you can retrieve periodically and fill in. A monthly report is a good example of a file that can be used as a template. The problem is that if you save the file with the same name it had when it was retrieved, the blank template is lost. The solution is to retrieve the template and fill it in, and then save the file with a different file name.

When you're ready to save the file, choose /File Save and then press Esc once to get rid of the original file name. Also, you can type a new name without pressing Esc. Now type a different name, like Septrept, and press Enter. The original template is still blank and ready for the next monthly report.

Problem 12:
You save a file by using an existing file name

This is one of those live-and-learn situations for which there is nothing you can do. After a file has been saved to disk, there is no unsaving it. If you used an existing name, the original data under that file name is lost. Keeping backups of your data is the best insurance against this problem.

Remember that every time you save a file using an existing file name, a

> **Backup**
>
> Consider choosing **Backup** from the **Cancel Replace Backup** options during saving. This choice renames the original file on disk with the same file name, but gives it a .BAK extension. If using that file name turns out to be a mistake for any reason, you can retrieve the .BAK file and get the original data back.

prompt appears that says Cancel Replace Backup. This warns you that you're using an existing file name. Choosing **R**eplace is the big mistake if you don't want to overwrite data on the disk.

Problem 13:
You save a file that includes very sensitive information and want to guarantee that no one will see it

You can save a file to disk and assign the file a password. Then, unless you type the password, you cannot retrieve the file.

To save a file with a password, press space bar and type P after the file name. After this, type the password you want to use. Make sure that your Caps Lock isn't on because passwords are case sensitive.

In other words, the password *HAPPY* is not the same as *happy*. Just to be sure you typed it right, you're prompted to type it again. The next time you try to retrieve the file, you're prompted to type the password. If you forget the password, the file is trapped forever on the disk, never again to see the light of day.

Problem 14:
You want only part of a file saved to the disk, but every time you save, the whole worksheet is saved

Using /File **X**tract allows you to save part of a worksheet under a different name. Part of this command requires you to decide whether you want to save formulas as formulas or just as the numbers they return. The reason? If the formula refers to cells that aren't being saved, it will return ERR. Be sure you use a new file name.

A Last Word on Files

Because Undo can't be used in file commands and because data loss is so devastating and permanent, it makes sense to understand these commands and use them carefully. If nothing else, be sure you save your work early and often. There is no substitute for this action.

You may also want to save your most important data to both your hard disk and a floppy disk. This way, you'll have a backup to your data just in case something happens to your hard disk. (Make sure you read Chapter 5 on how to prepare a 1-2-3 Survival Kit—you'll find some more tips on protecting yourself from devastating data loss.)

What To Do When...

Your Macros Won't Run

CHAPTER SEVENTEEN

Macros make using 1-2-3 so much easier. You can automate all the boring, repetitive things you have to do. You can also speed up your more complicated tasks.

Getting macros to work for you without having to do too much work on them is perhaps the highest-level skill in working with 1-2-3.

Macros under the Microscope

A macro is a series of recorded keystrokes. Things that you do repeatedly can be recorded so that you don't have to manually perform the same set of keystrokes every time. Complicated tasks you do can be automated so that you don't get mixed up or make a lot of mistakes. You can automate some keystrokes for less-skilled 1-2-3 users. Whatever the reason you write macros, you'll find they make using 1-2-3 much easier, smoother, and quicker.

Writing Macros

Macros are written in two ways. You can issue a command to 1-2-3 to remember the keystrokes you're about to do and then place them in your worksheet and call them a macro. Que's *Using 1-2-3* books have complete instructions for using the Learn feature to write macros.

The other way to write a macro is to move to a cell and type the commands for the macro. For example, you might need to go to individual cells all around your worksheet and format the values so that they look like money (the data is displayed with two decimal places and a dollar sign). The keystrokes for this task are /**R**ange **F**ormat **C**urrency **E**nter **E**nter. To write this as a macro, you would enter /RFC~~ in a cell. The curly line, called a *tilde*, is the symbol for the Enter key. The macro is almost complete.

Naming Macros

There is one more step to writing a macro. The cell with the macro in it has to be named. If it is not named, it is not a macro—it's just a cell with some stuff in it. To help you remember the names of macros you're naming, common practice is to type the name of the macro in the cell to the left. For example, you might write a macro in cell F1 and enter the macro name in cell E1. Entering the name in another cell is not necessary; the name simply reminds you of the names you used and tells you which keystrokes go with which name.

Putting a name in a cell is not naming a macro. You name a macro the way you name any range: Go to the cell storing the macro and choose /Range Name Create. Type a name, press Enter to finish the name, and press Enter again to choose that cell. The macro is named. You need to name only the first cell in a macro.

What name do you give to a macro? You have two choices here. You can use the backslash immediately followed by a letter, for example \f. The letter *F* reminds you that the macro formats cells.

.I Hereby Dub Thee...

A quicker way to name a macro goes like this. Go to the cell with the macro name in it, not the cell with the macro itself. Now choose /Range Name Labels Right. This uses the contents of the current cell as the name for the cell to the right. (Naturally, this assumes you put the name in a cell to the left of the macro.) Not only is this system faster, but you can also write a macro to name macros by using this set of keystrokes.

You can also give the macro a multi-character name, like format. Once the macro is named you can invoke it, meaning you can make the macro do its job. If you named a macro with backslash and a letter, you can invoke it easily. Just hold down the Alt key and press the letter of the macro. Alt+F would format the current cell with the currency format, showing two decimal places.

The multi-character name macros require an extra step to invoke. First press Alt+F3, type the name of the macro, and press Enter. If you have a lot of macros, you can press F3 (Names) to see a list of all your macros, highlight the one you want, and press Enter. Here is an example: To invoke the Format macro, go to the cell you want to format, press Alt+F3, and press F3 (Names) to see a list of all range names. Highlight the word FORMAT and press Enter.

Make It 27

Actually there are 27 possible Alt macros. You can also name a macro \0. An Alt+zero macro is automatically invoked whenever you retrieve the sheet it is in. To be really slick, try this: If you name one worksheet AUTO123.WK1, it will be automatically retrieved when you start 1-2-3. Put an Alt+zero macro in that worksheet and then exit 1-2-3. The next time you start 1-2-3, the worksheet appears and the macro executes automatically. Won't your coworkers be impressed!

You can see that the Alt+letter macros are easier to invoke, but of course you can have only 26 of them (because there are 26 letters).

A Column of Code

As long as there is macro code in the next cell down, your macro will run. Using many cells for your macros is much easier for several reasons. You can only enter 240 characters in a cell, so you might run into a wall before you're done entering an entire macro. Besides that, the macro is easier to read, and it is easier to fix. Imagine having to move left and right correcting macro errors in a 240-character label.

As you get used to writing macros, the time will come when you begin to write long macros. You don't have to write all the macro code in one cell. Enter just enough characters to be seen easily on the screen or enter the keystrokes for just one step in the macro. Then move down one cell and continue writing.

Running Macros

Just as a review, let's try writing a simple macro. It would be best to start with a blank worksheet just so you don't interfere with work you're doing in another sheet.

This macro will write your first name, move down one cell, and enter your last name. First, in cell A1, type the name you're giving to this macro. Call it \n (the n is for name, the letter you associate with the function of the macro). Before you type the backslash, enter an apostrophe. Without the apostrophe, the backslash will tell 1-2-3 to fill the cells with n's. So, if cell A1 is highlighted you should see ' \n.

In Cell B1 start to enter the macro code. Type your first name in cell B1. It's best not to enter the whole macro in one cell. Break it into smaller chunks by entering it in different cells (the next one down) so that if you need to edit it later on it will be a bit easier—not so much stuff in one cell. In cell B2 enter the instruction that moves the cell pointer down one cell—{down}. Note the beginning and ending curly braces; don't forget them.

In cell B3 enter your last name. You want 1-2-3 to press the Enter key for you so that your last name is entered in the cell. The macro symbol for the Enter key is the tilde (~), so type that after your last name.

Here's how it should look;

```
William          in cell B1
{down}           in cell B2
Shakespeare~     in cell B3
```

All that's left is to name and invoke the macro. Return to cell B1 and select /**R**ange **N**ame **C**reate. Type the name, \n, and press Enter to accept the name. Press Enter again to apply the name to cell B1.

Move to an empty cell away from the macro before you invoke it. To invoke the macro, hold down the Alt key and press the n key. Your first and last name should appear, first name above the last name.

Getting Your Macro in Step

Sometimes macros don't run quite the way you want them to. You missed a keystroke or entered some steps out of order. When that happens you can "step" through the macro. Stepping through a macro means that you execute it one keystroke at a time to see where the mistake is.

To step through a macro, press Alt+F2. Notice that a flag with the word STEP appears at the bottom of the screen. Now invoke the macro the normal way and press the space bar once for every keystroke in the macro. Watch the worksheet to see how the macro runs, and watch the area under the worksheet to see which keystroke is being executed.

10 Do's and Don'ts for Successful Macro Writing

1. *Do* go through the task you're going to automate and write down each keystroke.

2. *Don't* write the whole macro on one line.

3. *Do* plan your worksheet carefully so that macros won't interfere with data and vice versa.

4. *Don't* use keywords for names. Calc, the keyword for F9, is an example.

5. *Do* put a label prefix (an apostrophe) in front of macro code and use a backslash for macro names.

6. *Don't* skip rows when you're writing a macro in more than one row.

7. *Do* enter the macro name in a cell close to the macro, preferably to the left.

8. *Don't* put anything in a cell right under a macro. It becomes part of the macro.

9. *Do* be careful when you insert or delete rows. You might hurt your macros.

10. *Don't* automate something you're going to do only once. It isn't worth the time.

Making Your Macro Problems Go Away

Even if you don't write your own macros, you may be using a worksheet that includes macros written by somebody else. Whatever the case, if you run into problems running a macro, the following section provides some solutions.

Problem 1:
Only part of the macro executes

Chances are, you inserted a line that cracked open your macro. As long as the macro is in an unbroken column of cells, the whole thing will run. But when you use the /Worksheet Insert Row command and put a blank row in the middle of the macro, you've got problems. Another command that inserts a row is /Worksheet Page. This puts a blank row with a page break in the row above the cell pointer.

> ### Don't Touch Me!
>
> Macro code is like any other data placed in a worksheet. It can easily be deleted or changed. Once you have the macros working the way you want, you should consider protecting the cells where you put them so that they can't be deleted or changed. This won't prevent a row being inserted in the middle of a macro, but it makes other mistakes less likely.

Be sure that all lines of a macro are in one cell in the same column. Use as many cells as you like vertically, but once you jump columns your macro ends.

Problem 2:
Your macro empties a cell while it's executing

Very likely, somewhere in your macro code a space is lurking. Putting a space in some parts of a macro is like pressing the space bar and then Enter—it replaces the contents of a cell with a space. There are places where spaces are necessary in macros, but be careful where you use them.

Problem 3:
When you execute one macro, another macro executes too

I'll bet the bottom of the first macro is one cell above the first cell of the next one. This causes macro execution to continue right into the second macro. Be sure there is at least one line separating your macros.

To solve this problem, use /Worksheet Insert Row to separate the two macros. That may make a mess out of your data, though. The alternative is to move the second macro down one row.

Problem 4:
Your macros used to work fine, but now they don't. All you did was add some data to the area the macro acts on.

Check your macro code and be sure that all the cells the macro is supposed to affect are included in the macro. For instance, if you added new values to a range of numbers and the macro that formats them hasn't been changed, the macro will still work on the old values but not the new ones.

An example could be a macro that formats the values in cells A1 through A5. The macro was written specifically to format values in those cells. If you add values to cell A6, then, naturally that

Up-Up-Up-Up-Up and Away

If a macro needs to include cursor-movement commands, use {up} or {left} and so forth. {Down} moves the cell pointer down one cell. Typing {d} does the same. You could use {d}{d}{d}{d} to move down four cells, but it's faster to use {d 4}. One thing to keep in mind, though; put a space between the letter and number or the macro will think you typed a cell address. D4 in a macro is much different than {D 4}.

value won't be formatted by the macro until you change the macro to include that cell.

Problem 5:
You try invoking a macro, but you get beeped

You tried to invoke an Alt+letter macro you haven't named yet. Typing the name in the cell to the left isn't enough. You have to use /Range Name Create, type the name, the backslash, and the letter, and then press Enter twice. Be sure that you execute this command in the cell where the macro is, not in the cell storing the name.

Problem 6:
You try invoking a macro with a multi-character name and the Invalid Cell or Range Address error message appears

Again, the macro was not named. You can't just type the name in the cell to the left. You can name the macro by following the steps mentioned previously (in Problem 3). Another way is to put the cell pointer in the cell where you entered the name and choose /Range Name Labels Right.

Problem 7:
You try to use \a to name a macro and you get a cell full of aaaaaaaa instead

You forgot to start the macro name with an apostrophe. The backslash is a label prefix that repeats whatever you type next. Backslash in front of an *A* means the *A* is to be repeated until the cell is full.

Type the macro name again, but first type an apostrophe ('). If you're using a multi-character name, the apostrophe is supplied by 1-2-3, so you don't have to type it.

Problem 8:
You try to enter /RFC in a cell, but you keep calling up the commands

This is the same problem as Problem 7. If your macro starts with the slash key, which calls up the commands in the macro, you must start it with an apostrophe to tell 1-2-3 this is a label, and then type the slash. Otherwise, every time you press the slash key, you call up the commands. But then you found that out, didn't you? Remember, all macro code is made up of labels.

Problem 9:
You copy a macro to another place and change it, but the changes don't work

When you copy (rather than move) a macro, you leave the name behind. The old unchanged macro still has the name. If you copy and change a macro, you have to give the changed macro a new name. If you want to put a macro somewhere else in the worksheet, the best thing to do is move it. Then the name goes along.

Be careful about moving, though. If you moved any cell to the top line of the macro, the name is gone and it won't be recognized as a macro until you rename it. Remember that the name of a macro is only associated with the first cell of the macro.

Problem 10:
You write a fine macro. It runs great. But every time you add data, you have to edit the macro.

Instead of referring to ranges by cell addresses, refer to them by range name in macros. Expand a range when you add data. If more data is added to a range called Salary, for example, choose /Range Name Create and expand the range for this name. The macro that formats the range should be /RFC2~Salary~. This calls up the commands, executes /**R**ange Format Currency with two decimal places, and then makes it take place in the range called *Salary*. Because *Salary* has been expanded, all cells will be formatted.

Problem 11:

You write a macro, and when you invoke it, the screen goes crazy and won't stop

Sometimes you write a loop in your macro that repeats forever. Other times there is a bit of code that seems to jam things up. Whenever a macro seems out of control, you can stop it by pressing Ctrl+ Break. (The word *Break* is often cleverly concealed on the side of the Pause key.) To stop a macro, press both of these keys at the same time.

Problem 12:

You run a macro but it does its work in the wrong place

As in many software programs, it is necessary to place the cell pointer where you want the work to be done before you start the work. Therefore, if you want to format some cells over there (wherever there is), you have to move the cell pointer there, and then start the command. If the formatting is done through a macro, the same thing is true. Go to the place where the work is to be done and then run the macro.

Problem 13:

You typed the name of the macro but it didn't run

When a macro has a name (other than an Alt+key macro) you must press Alt+ F3 first, then the name of the macro. Alt+F3 tells 1-2-3 that you want to run a macro of a particular name. Be sure you type the name of the macro exactly right. Uppercase or lowercase doesn't matter, otherwise the name must be exact. If there is an underscore character in the name, for example, you must type that.

Remember that a macro lives in one worksheet. You can't retrieve another worksheet and expect a macro from another file to work there. The macro will have to be added to each sheet where you want to use it.

A Last Word on Macros

Macros in your worksheets are wonderful tools. They make life much easier, so you shouldn't be afraid of them. Start by writing a simple macro and add extra commands to it. Keep a reference handy like Que's *1-2-3 Beyond the Basics* or *1-2-3 Power Macros* to answer more complex questions when they arise.

What To Do When...

Your Graph Isn't There

CHAPTER EIGHTEEN

You've decided to create a graph. After all, a picture is worth a thousand words. But where is it? How come you can't see it? What are the tricks of the trade to making a graph appear in your worksheet and look the way you want it? This chapter explores those tricks and the pitfalls you may encounter.

Let's Get Graphic

You can add two kinds of graphs to your worksheet. The first are graphics that are already made and included on disk as part of the 1-2-3 program. These graphics are pictures of objects such as a telephone, a frame, or maps of parts of the world. The other kind of graph is the kind you create yourself. These can be artistic creative pictures or actual graphs based on your data.

The main menu (the one called up with the slash key) and the Wysiwyg menu (called up with the colon) both include Graph commands. The main menu is used to create data graphs and to add some features to those graphs. The Wysiwyg menu is used to create pictures and to add more creative elements to the data graphs. The Wysiwyg menu is also the one used to add a graph to a worksheet.

Graphing Data

After your worksheet is complete, the time has come to create the graph. If you add rows and columns of data after the graph is made, you have to go back to the Graph menu and modify some settings.

Call up the main Graph menu (/Graph) and notice that the next menu includes the letters X, A, B, C, D, E, and F. The data you want to graph must be assigned to a specific data range in the graph. The labels—for example, people's names—would be the X range. The first column or row of numerical data associated with those names you want to graph becomes range A, the next becomes range B, and so forth, for up to six ranges of numbers.

A worksheet might list the names of salespeople in column A. All the names would be assigned to the X range. The data in the worksheet shows their sales performance for various products offered by the company. Their performance on up to six products can be included in the graph.

The actual graph shows the X range (the names of the salespeople) along the x-axis, which is the horizontal line along the bottom of the graph. Each number associated with each salesperson becomes a point on a line (in a line graph) or a bar (in a bar graph). There can be up to six points or bars per person.

The length of each bar or the height of each point above the x-axis is measured along the y-axis. The scale of the y-axis is determined by the highest number in the graphed data.

After the data has been assigned to a range, you can view the graph. Anytime you want to see the graph, press F10 (Graph)

Hurry Up!

Usually all the data you want to include in a graph is entered in adjacent columns or rows. If this is the case, you don't have to highlight each data range separately. Speed things up by using /Graph Group. You can highlight the whole range of data you want included in the graph. You have to choose columnwise or rowwise, depending on whether you arranged data below the labels (rowwise) or to the right of the labels (columnwise). All the ranges are assigned with a minimum of keystrokes.

and the graph you created fills the screen. At this point, the graph is not in the worksheet; it is simply a graph associated with the worksheet. The next section deals with how graphs are added to worksheets.

Graphs are interactive with data. Notice that when you change a number, the graph part that displays that number changes. There are some times when this is not good. When you have a large worksheet with the graph added to it, changing a number may make everything stop while the graph updates, and this may be a couple of seconds. To prevent this from

More Speed!

Another way to speed things up is to choose :Graph Settings Display No. Instead of a graph, you'll see a shaded area.

happening, use :Graph Settings Sync No. The graph will not update until you choose :Graph Compute. Don't forget to use this command before you print; otherwise, your graph will be out-of-date.

You might need to create several graphs. Each graph may be based on different data in the worksheet, or you might choose another graph type to make another point about the data.

When you create several graphs, be sure to name each one of them. Any name up to 15 characters will do. One might be Sales_bar and another could be Pie. Any name that helps you remember what the graph is about will do.

After graphs are named, you can create new ones, call up other named graphs and work on them, or add any of them to the worksheet.

Graphs can also be saved. Using the /Graph Save command is like taking a snapshot of the graph displayed on-screen. Enhancements you may have added to the graph with the

---

PrintGraph No More!

In the past, it was necessary to save a graph if you wanted to print it. The only way to print graphs in earlier releases of 1-2-3 (before Release 2.2 or 3.1) was to exit the program and enter another Lotus program called PrintGraph. Graphs could not be added to worksheets, so they had to be printed separately. That is no longer necessary.

Wysiwyg menu will not be saved, however. If you change data, the saved graph will not change unless you save it again. Saving is the only way to create an actual file of the graph on disk. The file is saved with the name you type and the .PIC extension.

Adding Graphs to the Worksheet

Until you add the graph to the worksheet, you can view it only by pressing F10 (Graph) or choosing the /Graph View command. After the graph is in the worksheet, it is visible all the time and can be printed with the data. Use the Wysiwyg menu to add a graph to a worksheet.

Choose :Graph Add and then choose the kind of graph you want to add. There are five kinds of graphs that you can add to a worksheet:

Current. Whatever graph you're working on now is the current graph. If you've not created a graph, an empty graph is placed in the target range. When you do create a graph, it is placed in this range.

Named. You place in the worksheet the different graphs you created and named by using this command.

PIC. Any graph you saved can be added when you pick this option.

Metafile. The graphics that PIC come with the 1-2-3 program, with Lotus SmartPics, or from any file with the extension CGM (Computer Graphics Metafile) are added to the worksheet with this option.

Blank. A blank graph is one you would add to a worksheet if you planned to create a picture of your own. After the graph is added, you choose :Graph Edit and press Enter when the cell pointer is somewhere in the blank graph. Now add your own artwork to the blank graph with the new menu you see at the top of the screen.

Making Pictures

Not all graphs are based on data. You can add a blank graph to a worksheet and then edit it, adding lines, freehand drawings, and colors.

To add a blank graph to the worksheet, choose :Graph Edit in the range where you placed that blank graph and you're now able to add text, lines, polygons, arrows, rectangles, ellipses, and freehand drawings. You

---

Do Yourself a Favor

The task of adding lines, arrows, and other Wysiwyg features to graphs is made much easier when you use a mouse. It is possible to do all these things without a mouse, of course, but being able to click on menu items, place objects, and drag lines and shapes around the graph is a great deal faster with a mouse.

---

can also move your drawings around and color them, slant them, flip them, and increase the size of the text you added.

The *Using 1-2-3* series from Que describes in detail the steps used to create and enhance 1-2-3 graphics.

10 Do's and Don'ts for Working with Graphs

1. *Do* add the graph to an area of the worksheet where data you need to see will not be hidden.

2. *Don't* put the graph in a range that is too small or too large.

3. *Do* set the options to Black and White if you plan to print the graph in black and white.

4. *Don't* add a saved graph to a worksheet if you want it to change when you change data.

5. *Do* remember that each type of graph is used to make different points about your data. Choose the graph type carefully.

6. *Don't* forget to reassign graph data ranges if you add more cells to or delete cells from ranges in your worksheet.

7. *Do* use the F3 (Names) key when selecting one graph among several in a single cell for editing, moving, or removing.

8. *Don't* forget to save your worksheet after creating graphs, even if you don't add them to the worksheet. All their settings will be lost.

9. *Do* use **:Graph Settings Display No** or **:Graph Settings Sync No** if it takes a lot of time for your graph to update after you change data.

10. *Don't* be surprised if changes you make with some main menu commands don't appear in the graph you added. You may have to remove it and add it again to the worksheet.

Fixing Graph Problems

Here are some of the things that typically go wrong when graphs are added to worksheets.

Problem 1:
You add a graph, but you don't see it

There are several causes for this very common problem:

- *If you added a current graph but did not create a graph, there is no graph to add.* Call up the main Graph menu and check the settings sheet to be sure that there are cells assigned to the various ranges. You may have accidently used /Graph **Reset Ranges**, which clears all the range settings you worked so hard to make. If no ranges are set, you must reassign all the data ranges to a letter range.

- *If you added a blank graph, you'll not see a data-based graph.* This type of graph is used for creating tailor-made graphic drawings. Add the current graph or a named graph.

- *If you added a graph to a single cell, it is so small it may look like a smudge.* Use **:Graph Settings R**ange to put the graph in a range that covers more than one cell.

- *If you added a graph to a range that is too large, the main part of the graph may be off-screen.* Again, use **:Graph Settings Range**. Put the graph in a range that is smaller than the entire screen.

Problem 2:
You add a graph, but all you get is a shaded area

From the Wysiwyg menu, choose **:Graph Settings Display Yes**. Somehow, the **Display No** option had been chosen and that means the graph is replaced with a shaded area.

Problem 3:
You add a graph and the data behind it shows through

Choose :Graph Settings Opaque Yes. When a graph is not opaque, whatever is in the cells behind it can be seen through the graph. Sometimes that is desirable. If the data and graph are not arranged properly, however, the display is very confusing.

Problem 4:
You try to view a graph, but nothing works

The way to see a graph you've created when it has not been added to the sheet is to use /Graph View or press the F10 (Graph) key. A picture of your graph fills the screen. This step assumes that you've correctly created a graph. If you're using a computer without a graphics card, displaying a graph is impossible. You'll need to upgrade your computer system to display graphics in order to see your 1-2-3 graphs.

Spend the Money

Today you can buy a VGA graphics card for about $100 and a nice color monitor for about twice that price. It's worth the expenditure.

If the graph view screen appears but there's no graph, it is entirely possible that you've not yet assigned ranges and their data to the graph letter ranges (X, A, B, and so forth).

Remember that the F10 key or /Graph View command is for graphs based on worksheet data only. You cannot use them to see blank graphs or metafiles added with the Wysiwyg command.

Problem 5:
You add a graph to the worksheet and the control panel says it's there, but you can't see it

Be sure that you're in Wysiwyg graphics display mode. Graphs can not be seen in text mode. Use :Display Mode Graphics to switch to graphics mode.

If this is not the problem, be sure that the graph you want to see is the only graph in the cell. If you overlap graphs, one will interfere with the display of the other. When several graphs are in the same cell, they are all listed in order of placement.

Problem 6:
You add a .PIC or .CGM file to the worksheet, but you can't see it

You can trick 1-2-3 with this command, or it can trick you. Start by choosing :Graph Add PIC or Metafile and typing the name of a file. Highlight the range and press Enter and the upper part of the screen assures you that the graph is in the range. You can type the name of a graph that doesn't exist and 1-2-3 will still show that a graph of that name has been placed in that range. Because the graph doesn't exist, you can't see it. For this reason, be sure that you get the path (the drive and directory) and the name of the file exactly right, or you'll be displaying a nonexistent graph.

Getting Rid of a Graph

To remove a graph, use :Graph Remove. The only way to be sure you remove the right graph is to press F3 (Names) and choose the one you want to remove. To move a graph, choose :Graph Move; again, use F3 to choose the right graph, and then press Enter. Move the key to the upper left corner of the new range for the graph you're moving and press Enter. The graph is moved.

Problem 7:

You have a graph in your worksheet, but it won't print

First, be sure the graph is included in the print range. If it isn't completely included, only the part of the graph included in the print range will appear on the printout.

Also, be sure you're using the Wysiwyg Print menu (invoked with the colon key). The main print menu (invoked with the slash) will not print any Wysiwyg enhancements, including a graph.

A Last Word on Adding Graphs

A printout of a worksheet that has a graph included is a professional document indeed. Check the graph carefully on-screen and in the printout to be sure that the point you're trying to make is stated clearly by the graph. When printing, it is especially important that the display of the graph and the data don't interfere with one another.

Your Graph Looks Wrong

CHAPTER NINETEEN

Creating a graph from the numbers you've entered in your worksheet makes it much easier to see what the numbers mean. Are profits up? What are the trends? Where are the weak spots? Questions like these are easier to answer when you can look at a graph.

But if the graph is not well planned, it can raise as many questions as it is intended to answer. This chapter helps you identify ways you can improve your graphs.

Searching for Meaning

No thinking person would simply highlight some data, create a pie graph, print it, and distribute it without being sure everyone knows what the graph represents. Using the main graph menu and the Wysiwyg graph menu, you can make your message crystal clear.

As we've stated previously, you access the main graph menu with the slash key and the Wysiwyg graph menu with the colon. This section provides a rundown of the changes you can make to your graph using these two menus.

In the Main

To access the main graph menu, choose /Graph. You use the main graph menu to do the following:

Create the graph. See Chapter 18 for an overview of creating graphs, or refer to Que's *Using 1-2-3* for a more detailed description.

Choose the type of graph. Each type makes a different point. For instance, use bar graphs to compare data to other data. Use pie graphs to show how each piece of data contributes to the whole. Use line graphs to show trends.

Name and save the graph. Naming enables you to create several graphs for a worksheet. Saving enables you to save a graph to a disk.

A Table of Elements

Here are some elements from the Options menu that you can use to punch up your graph:

Titles are generally short phrases that state the purpose of the graph. You can use up to two separate titles.

Legends explain the meaning of each bar or design used for data in the graph.

Grid places horizontal lines, vertical lines, or both in the graph so it is easier to see the position of the data points compared to the Y-axis.

Data-Labels identify each marker in line graphs.

B&W or **Color** display is chosen to suit the monitor you're using or to change the display so that it looks more like the printout.

Add elements to the graph. The /**Graph O**ptions menu enables you to add such enhancements as legends, titles, a grid, and data labels. You can also change the graph from color to black and white and change the scale for the y-axis.

What's with Wysiwyg?

To access the Wysiwyg graph menu, choose **:G**raph. You use the Wysiwyg graph menu to do the following:

Add the graph to the worksheet

Remove the graph from the worksheet

Move the graph to a different range

Change the size of the display in the worksheet

Goto the graph you've added to your worksheet

Edit the graph

The **:G**raph **E**dit menu has a large selection of additions and changes you can make to your graph. For example,

You can add text. This means that in addition to the titles, legends, and data-labels you added, you can create and place other bits of text in the graph.

You can create and place lines, arrows, polygons, rectangles, ellipses, and freehand drawings in the graph.

You can change the color, size, slant, and orientation of many graph elements and the font magnification of the text in the graph.

You can add a grid.

With all these features, it's easy to become confused and make mistakes. The following Do's and Don'ts list can help you avoid the most common mistakes as you work with the graph menus.

10 Do's and Don'ts for Enhancing Graphs

1. *Do* use titles and legends to explain your graph.

2. *Don't* forget that it's easier to use cell references than to type the text for legends and data-labels.

3. *Do* change to **:Display** Mode **B&W** to see the graph as it will look in a black-and-white printout.

4. *Don't* squeeze a graph into too small a range in the worksheet because it makes the graph difficult to read.

5. *Do* use **/Graph** Options Scale Skip and change the setting if the tick marks on the y-axis are too close.

6. *Don't* forget to use **:Graph** Compute if you set **:Graph** Settings Sync to **No**.

7. *Do* seriously consider using a mouse when you enter the Wysiwyg menu to change graphs.

8. *Don't* expect .PIC files that you added to a sheet to update when you change data.

9. *Do* create a special B data range for use with pie graphs.

10. *Don't* try to include negative numbers in a pie graph; there is no such thing as a negative piece of pie.

Solving Graph Problems

You've created a graph and placed it in your worksheet, but now there are things about it you don't like. This section lists some common problems and tells you which menu items can help correct these problems.

Problem 1:
You don't know what the bars or lines represent

This is where a legend comes to the rescue. A bar graph with six bars per cluster is pretty hard to figure out unless you use /Graph Options Legend. Type a description for each data range. For example, if you're comparing the sales of six products for each salesperson, each bar stands for a product. The legend tells which product is associated with which data range.

After assigning legends, view the graph. At the bottom of the graph is a box that shows the color or design of each line or bar and a descriptive label.

> **Quicker and Slicker**
>
> The best way to assign text to your graph using the main graph menu is to use the cell address of the text rather than typing the text. For example, if the main title will be the same as the text you entered in cell D1, choose /Graph Options Titles First. At the prompt, instead of typing what's in the cell, just type \D1. Notice that if you change the contents of D1, the title changes automatically.
>
> This same procedure works with legends. You can use a cell address with a backslash instead of typing the text for each legend. For example, if the legend for a particular item in the X range is in cell A4, at the legends prompt, type /A4. The advantage to using cell addresses is that you can change the data in the worksheet and the legends will change automatically.

Problem 2:
Some clusters have more bars than others

Check your data ranges in the graph settings box, which appears when you enter the /Graph menu. Each data range (A, B, C, and so forth) should be assigned the same number of cells.

Check your data ranges by choosing :Graph Settings.

If you highlighted too few or too many cells for some ranges, press the letter of the data range that has the incorrect range, then highlight the proper range.

Problem 3:
Lines or bars are the wrong height

It is difficult to compare two numbers in a graph if one is much larger than another. If this happens, you have two choices. One method is to create two graphs. One graph features the smaller numbers and the other features the larger ones.

The second alternative is to change the Y-scale. Choose /Graph Options Scale Y-Scale. If you want to determine the lower and upper limits, set the scale to manual. In this way, the graph features data only in the specified ranges. Be careful of this action, though. Sometimes data that is much lower in value than the rest of the data might be represented by graph elements (bars for example) so short that they have no meaning. Data much higher in value may be represented by graph elements that hit the top of the graph and don't show its true value.

Y Reformat?

If the appearance of the numbers listed next to the y-axis don't look the way you want them to, choose /Graph Options Y-Scale Format. Now you can format those numbers in the same way that you format numbers in the worksheet.

If you change the Y-scale, some of the numbers in your graph ranges might not display correctly. Either the low numbers or the high ones will not be accurate. Again, it might be necessary to create two graphs, each with a different Y-scale setting.

Problem 4:
The graph titles, legends, and data-labels are too small

The solution to this problem depends on how you want your final worksheet to look. You could increase the range where you're displaying the graph. Use :Graph Settings Range and increase the display range. A bigger graph means bigger text in the graph.

If that is not possible, use :Graph Edit Options Font-Magnification. A value larger than 100 increases the size of the letters. You can set numbers from 0% to 1000% magnification.

Problem 5:
The text added with :Graph Edit Add Text is too large

For text you added with Wysiwyg, you can change the font with :Graph Edit Edit Font. Choose among the standard eight fonts available in Wysiwyg. Highlight the text you want to change and press Enter.

> **And Furthermore ...**
>
> You can change the appearance of a character or word in text by using formatting. Chapter 7 describes this in detail, but here's a brief explanation. Start typing text to add to a graph or a cell. When you get to the word that you want to format differently, press Ctrl+A, enter the formatting code, type the word, then press Ctrl+N. Using this technique, you can change, for example, one word in a phrase to bold or italic.

Problem 6:
All the pieces in your pie graph are separate

A pie graph is unique among graphs. It can display only one data range, the A range. Each item in the X range gets one piece of pie for its number in the A range.

It is possible to have a B range in pie graphs, but you don't get a second piece of pie. Instead, you get a color or a pattern inside each piece. This is the way you fill pie pieces. The best technique is to use a special B range just for the pie graph and make each cell a single digit. Now each piece will have a unique pattern or color.

Here is an extra trick. Substitute a number over 100 for a single digit in the data for the B range, and the piece of pie it corresponds to will *explode* or stand out from the rest of the pie. Sometimes you forget to change the B range from *real* data to a special range of single digits when using a pie graph. Then all pieces explode. Remember, though, if you specify a special B range for a pie graph and later switch back to another type of graph with more than one data range, you must switch the B range back to *real* data.

Problem 7:
Your graph looks squashed or stretched

There are two possible causes. One is that you changed the Y-axis and now it appears strange because the longer bars or higher lines are at the top of the graph. Choose /Graph Options Scale Y-Scale Automatic to let 1-2-3 set the scale.

The more likely cause is that you placed the graph in your worksheet in a range that is not suited to the shape of the graph. Experiment with other ranges; use fewer cells in one direction or more cells in the other direction. For instance, if you added a graph to cells A10 to G15, the graph may be too long for its height. Choose :Graph Settings Range. Extend the range downward and then see how the graph looks.

Some People Are Never Satisfied

If you're never satisfied, you'll be happy to know that you can change lots of other things about the graph if you explore the menu. Use :Graph Edit Edit (yes, the two *Edits* are correct) to change fonts, line styles, line widths, the location and number of arrowheads, the centering of labels, the roundness of corners in objects you add to a graph, and the colors of all the graph elements. You can even change the eight colors available to you by using :Graph Edit Color Map.

Problem 8:
The named graph in the worksheet doesn't update

For example, suppose you create a graph, and add a grid by using /Graph Options Grid. You then name the graph and add it to the worksheet. Later, you go back to the main menu and remove the grid. The graph in the worksheet, however, still has the grid. This happens with named graphs added to the sheet, but not with current graphs. Current graphs added to a sheet change as commands are issued.

The way to solve this problem is to rename the graph. Choose :Graph Name Create, and use the same name you used before. Press Enter, and the changes appear in the graph in the sheet.

Problem 9:
The graph looks awful when you print it

I'll bet you have a color monitor and a black ink printer. What looks good in color may not look so good in black and white.

To guarantee an acceptable printed graph, choose :Graph Options B&W in the main menu, which makes your graph display as a black-and-white graph. Colors are changed to designs of lines and dots.

> ### XY Pains
>
> As you explore the graph menu, you'll probably try the XY graph type option to see what that graph looks like. You may be surprised to see all the lines pressed against the left side of the graph.
>
> This happens because the XY graph type is unique in that it alone uses numbers, not labels, in the X range. An XY graph is used specifically to compare one set of numbers to another set of numbers. Set a range of values into the X range and try it again.

If you also want to change your whole display to black and white, choose :Display Mode B&W. Then, while in this display mode, highlight a print range that includes the graph. Choose :Print Preview, and see if the graph looks good on-screen.

Problem 10:
The graph changed when you chose /Graph Options Format Graph area

That's how area graphs work. In a line graph, for example, each line is displayed relative to the other lines. If one point on a line represents 60 and a corresponding point on another line represents 70, the point for 70 is higher than the one for 60. If you change to area graphs, however, the results are stacked, one on top of the other.

If this is a problem, use the main graph menu again. Choose :Graph Options Format Graph **Both** to remove the stacked area formatting. The **Both** option creates a graph with a design at each data point and a line connecting those points.

Dangerous Area

Be careful if you use /Graph Options Format Graph Area on only certain data ranges. Some lines in the graph will be stacked; other lines will zig and zag around the stacked areas. When a graph is stacked, each value is piled on top of the one below it. If two lines represent a 60 and a 70, the line corresponding to the 70 will be 70 points higher in the graph than the line corresponding to the 60. If there were another unstacked line representing a 50, it would be placed in the graph even with its true value. The result can be mind-boggling.

Problem 11:
Editing graphs in that little window is too hard

Choose :Graph Edit View. Properly used, this menu lets you zoom in and concentrate on a small part of your graph, allowing more precise editing. It's like getting a germ's eye view of your graph. You have the following choices:

Full returns you to the regular editing window.

In enables you to highlight a section of the graph and see it up close.

Pan enables you to move back and forth, move up and down, and zoom in on certain areas of the graph.

+ and − enable you to zoom into or out of the current screen area.

Up, Down, Left, and Right move the focus area one-half screen in the stated direction.

A Last Word on Enhancing Your Graphs

Before you create a presentation quality worksheet complete with a graphic, it is a good idea to become familiar with the menus and choices available to you. If nothing else, the graph menus of the program are especially fun to play with when the boss isn't watching.

Little Things Become Major Aches and Pains

CHAPTER TWENTY

This chapter is a catchall. Problems and questions which don't fit into one of the other chapters are included here. For a smoother 1-2-3 session, be sure you also check out Chapter 23, "The Great 1-2-3 Trouble-shooting Road Map."

Onward and Upward

The name 1-2-3 was chosen because the program has three important capabilities. It is, first and foremost, a spreadsheet. It can also be used as a database, and it can create graphics.

You can expand the usefulness of the program, however, beyond these three areas with knowledge of the menus, a grasp of macro procedures, a growing awareness of advanced features, and an understanding of page layout. For example, you can use 1-2-3 as a word processor using the Wysiwyg :Text Edit menu. You can create forms, resumes, slide shows, and presentation-quality documents using Wysiwyg, macros, and some ingenuity.

As you learn more about what you can do with 1-2-3, you'll learn more about what can go wrong with 1-2-3. That's what this chapter is about. So if you're experiencing some off-the-wall 1-2-3 problems, read on!

A Shameless Plug

New questions will arise as you expand your capabilities. New needs will surface as you create more complex worksheets with fancier enhancements. That's why this *Oops!* book is just one of many 1-2-3 books published by Que.

When you want to expand your 1-2-3 horizons, head down to your local retailer and browse through the section of big black books on 1-2-3 from Que. From *Using 1-2-3* to *1-2-3 Power Macros*, you'll find a new world of 1-2-3 information that will help you get more out of your favorite worksheet program.

10 Do's and Don'ts for Using 1-2-3

1. *Do* use the **:Text Edit** feature when you must enter a lot of text in several lines.

2. *Don't* forget to use the Update part of the Default menu in **/Worksheet Global Default** and **:Display Default** to make your changes permanent.

3. *Do* use a label prefix before a complicated formula so that if the formula is rejected, you can enter it in a cell and edit it.

4. *Don't* be afraid to use the add-ins, which are powerful tools.

5. *Do* remember the shortcut keys. For example, use F10 to view a graph or F7 to repeat a data query command. And Ctrl-Break is much better than lots of Esc keypresses.

6. *Don't* forget **/Worksheet Global Default Other International** when you're dissatisfied with punctuation in values, the display of dates or times, or the currency symbol.

7. *Do* save your work frequently.

8. *Don't* feel obliged to squeeze your data into a tiny area, but also be careful not to spread it over too large an area with lots of empty areas—especially if your computer lacks adequate memory.

9. *Do* have the Undo feature on whenever possible. Chapter 5 tells you how to use this feature.

10. *Don't* trust your luck. Save your work early and often.

Correcting Some Common Problems

As you explore the fringes of 1-2-3, or as you try new aspects of the old familiar menu, you may encounter some problems. Here are some things that deserve your attention.

Winkin' and Blinkin'

If the blinking hardware cursor bothers you, choose **:Display Options Adapter Blink No**. Don't forget to choose **:Display Default Update** if you want to make the change permanent.

Problem 1:
The beep bugs you

Choose **/Worksheet Global Default Other Beep No**. The beep is silenced.

Problem 2:
You want to use a foreign currency symbol

Again, this is a case for the Worksheet menu. Choose **/Worksheet Global Default Other International Currency** and type the currency symbol. How do you type it? Read Problem 3.

Problem 3:
The characters you want are not on the keyboard

As you use 1-2-3, you occasionally may need to type characters that are not on the keyboard. The default currency symbol is the dollar sign, and of course it is on the keyboard. But what about yen, or rupee, or pound sterling? If each currency symbol had its own key, there wouldn't be any space left for letters and numbers.

There are two ways to create less common characters, such as currency symbols: using LICS characters or using compose sequences. Check the back of the 1-2-3 documentation for a list of these characters.

LICS stands for Lotus International Character Set. To produce a non-keyboard character, you type @char(*number*), in which *number* represents the LICS number for the character you want. For instance, @char(163) produces the pound sterling symbol.

The other way to add non-keyboard characters to your worksheet is with compose sequences. Press Alt+F1, then type two characters; the two characters are placed in the same space. For instance, to produce the cent sign you can press Alt+F1, and then type C and | (the *pipe* symbol, sometimes shown as ¦ on your keyboard).

Problem 4:

You type a non-keyboard character and a number, but the cell entry is a label

You can't use compose sequences or LICS characters in values. For example, you can't type @char(163)100 for 100 pounds. If the cell entry must be a value, type the symbol in one column, narrow the column to one character, and then type the amount in the next column to the right.

Playing with Strings

A string is a series of characters that is treated as a label by 1-2-3. In 1-2-3, you can concatenate (put together) several strings in one cell. To do so, you create a special formula. Start with a plus sign. Type literal strings in quotation marks, with an ampersand (&) between strings. Type formulas without quotation marks.

For example, to produce the phrase *Tickets are 17 £*, type

+"Tickets are 17 "&@char(**163**)

Problem 5:

You press an arrow key, but the cell pointer doesn't move and the whole screen shifts

You accidentally pressed the Scroll Lock key. Press it again to turn scroll lock off.

Problem 6:
The screen clock is wrong

No Clock, Please

At the bottom of your screen, you can elect to see the clock, the file name of the current worksheet, or nothing. Choose /Worksheet Global Default Other Clock. Then choose either None, Clock, or Filename.

You don't set the clock in 1-2-3. Use the /System command to suspend 1-2-3 temporarily. At the DOS prompt, type Time and press Enter. Type the time, using the syntax HH:MM:SS and press Enter. (Use military time if it is the afternoon. For example, 1:00 P.M. is entered as 13:00.) Type Exit to return to 1-2-3.

Problem 7:
You don't know how to place a value from another worksheet file into the current sheet

This would be a great time to learn about the Viewer add-in. Attach it by choosing /Addin Attach, typing Viewer or highlighting its name and pressing Enter. Choose the next available number in the menu that begins No Key..., and then choose Quit.

Linking and Copying

After linking one cell from another sheet to the current sheet, you can link other cells by copying the first cell you linked. Copying the cell down one row will bring to the current sheet the cell that is below the one originally linked.

For example, suppose you linked cell A1 from another file to cell E1 in the current sheet. If you copy cell E1 to E2, the contents of A2 from the other file will be in E2 of the current sheet.

Go to an empty cell and simultaneously press Alt and the number you chose in the menu. If you chose 8, for instance, you would press Alt+F8 to start Viewer.

Choose Link from the menu that appears, because you want to bring the contents of one cell into the current sheet. All the files in the current directory are listed. Highlight the one you want to link to, press the right-arrow key, move the cell pointer to the cell you want to link to the current sheet, and press Enter.

After you link, you'll notice that changing the cell in the current file will change if you have changed the linked cell in the other sheet. To force the link to update, choose /File Admin Link-Refresh. Be careful if you delete the other file, because the current cell will eventually return ERR.

To prevent the formula from updating, choose /Range Value and press Enter twice. This converts the formula to a value, which prevents it from updating.

If you don't want to use Viewer, you can write the following formula to link a cell to an offsheet cell

> +<<*pathname\filename*>>cell addresss or range name

in which *pathname* is the drive and directory for the file you're linking, *filename* is the name of the file you're linking, and *cell* is the cell you want linked into the current sheet.

Problem 8:
You can't enter a date later than 1999 using @DATE

Yes you can. The normal format for this formula is

> @DATE(YY,MM,DD)

For years 2000 and beyond, use three digits for the year. For example, use 100 for 2000, or use 101 for 2001.

Problem 9:
You don't want to type the dates for the next year

Any time you need to enter a series of values in a range, consider using the /Data Fill command. It works for any values, including dates.

Suppose you want to list all Mondays for the rest of the year. Put your cell pointer in the top cell of the range where you want the dates entered. Choose /Data Fill. Anchor the cell pointer and high-light downward at least 52 cells (there are 52 Mondays). After you press Enter, a menu appears that includes Start, Step, and Stop. At the Start prompt, type

@DATE(YY,MM,DD)

for the first Monday in the year. At the Step prompt, type 7 because there are seven days between Mondays. At the Stop prompt, type

@DATE(YY,MM,DD)

substituting the year, month, and date for the last Monday in the year. Press Enter and five-digit numbers fill the range.

Convert the display of those numbers to dates by choosing /Range Format Date and choosing the date format you want. Highlight all the cells and you have a column of Mondays.

This exercise illustrates that there are faster ways to do many operations in 1-2-3. Data fill takes a lot of drudgery out of data entry, and combining the command with other techniques gives quick and accurate results.

Problem 10:
You were switched to EDIT mode while typing a complicated formula

After you begin entering a formula, you have to get it right, or it will be rejected when you press Enter. You usually don't want to leave the formula in the control panel, unable to enter it in a cell, until you get it right. You have other things to do.

As it says in the do's and don'ts, put a label prefix in front of a troublesome formula if you want to get it into a cell. It won't process any data because it's a label. But it's better to enter a wrong label than to press Esc and start writing the formula all over again.

When it's time to edit the formula, remember to press F2 (Edit). You can use Ctrl+right-arrow or the Tab key to move five characters to the right. Ctrl+left-arrow or Shift+Tab moves five characters to the left. Home takes the cursor to the beginning or left end of the formula, and End takes the cursor to the right end.

To get help, remove the label prefix, put the cursor in the part of the formula you need help with, and press F1 (Help). If you need help with an @IF formula, for example, put the cursor somewhere on *IF* and press F1.

Problem 11:
You need to enter a paragraph. Guessing when to stop one line and start the next is a pain.

Choose **:Text Edit** and highlight as far to the right and down as you want. The range you highlight determines the area in which the text will appear.

The cell pointer changes to a vertical bar called the *insertion point.* You simply type; the text fills the range to the right and wraps to the next line. When you're finished typing, press Esc.

Problem 12:
:Text Reformat doesn't change the paragraph you entered with :Text Edit

You use **:Text Reformat** to fit into a new range the text you typed with **:Text Edit**. If the new range is not as wide as the old range, **:Text** Reformat does not seem to work. The reason is simple. All the cells in which you entered text have a {TEXT} attribute associated with them. Move the cell pointer to cell A1 and look above the worksheet in the control panel and you'll see A1: {TEXT}.

When you use **:Text Reformat** to fit text in a narrower range, the existing text spreads into all the cells to the right that have the text attribute. The solution? Get rid of the attribute in the cells where you don't want text. Choose :Text Clear, highlight the necessary cells, and press Enter. Now perform the :Text Reformat, highlighting the cells where you want the text to be placed; the text fills the new smaller range.

Put It on the Table

Another table you might find useful is a list of all the files on a disk or in a particular directory. Choose /File Admin Table, then highlight the type of file you want listed. The upper left corner of the resulting table will be the cell where the cell pointer is currently placed. For each file, the table lists the file name, size, date, and time of the most recent update.

Problem 13:
You forget which range names you used or which ranges go with which names

Choose /Range Name Table in an empty range. All the names you used are listed, along with their ranges.

Problem 14:
While using Macro Library Manager, you load a library of macros and some don't work

When you choose Load from the menu in Macro Library Manager, you bring into the computer's memory a library of macros you saved at another time. That library might have a macro with the same name as a macro in the current sheet. The macro in the sheet supersedes the macro in the library. For example, if your sheet has a \b macro that enters the current date in the cell, and the library has a \b macro that erases the current cell, you'll see the current date in the cell.

The solution is to go to an empty range and invoke Macro Library Manager. This is done with /Addin Invoke or Alt+the function key you chose when you first attached Macro Library Manager. Choose Edit from the Macro Library Manager menu that appears after you invoke the macro manager, highlight the library you want to edit, press Enter, and choose Overwrite to place the macros in your worksheet. Now change the names of any macros to something you haven't used in the current sheet and save the macro library.

A Last Word on Miscellany

You can stretch your knowledge of 1-2-3 by using the help feature, trying new ways to do the routine tasks, and experimenting with new areas of the program. Don't be afraid to try new things. Eventually, you'll become the local expert everyone turns to for help with problems and questions.

A Quick Course in Problem Solving

Examining the Versions and Releases of 1-2-3

CHAPTER TWENTY-ONE

1-2-3 is three applications in one: a spreadsheet, a database, and a graphics program. It's easy to get confused about all the different versions and releases of 1-2-3 on the market. This chapter clears up the mystery about which is which.

Releases and Versions

A *version* of 1-2-3 is a copy of the program used with a particular type of computer or operating environment. There is one version of 1-2-3 for the Mac, and several versions for the IBM PC and compatibles.

One version for the IBM PC and compatibles is called 1-2-3 for Windows. This version can be run only under the Windows operating environment. Another version of 1-2-3 is used on OS/2, an alternative operating system to DOS for PCs. Yet another version for IBM PC and compatibles works directly from DOS. Although you can use this version also within Windows, it does not have all the capabilities of 1-2-3 for Windows. For example, you cannot cut to and paste from the clipboard.

A *release* is an improvement of another release in a version. The major releases of 1-2-3 for DOS are 1A, 2.0, 2.01, 2.2, 2.3, 2.4, 3.0, 3.1, 3.1+, 3.4, and 1-2-3 for Home.

What Do the Numbers Mean?

Notice that all but two of the releases begin with 2 or 3. The 2 means the worksheet is two-dimensional. A two-dimensional worksheet has a working area with width (256 columns) and length (8192 rows). Everything entered in the cells is placed in this area.

A 3 on a release means the product is three-dimensional. The worksheet is the same length and width as a two-dimensional worksheet, but it also has a third dimension, called *sheets*. There are 256 possible sheets in the three-dimensional world of 1-2-3. This means you could have 256 separate worksheets, each with 256 columns and 8192 rows. That's a lot of cells and a lot of data, and it requires a lot of memory.

With 3.x releases, you can create data ranges that spread out in three dimensions rather than two. You can also write formulas that process numbers from any cell in any sheet.

One release that does not begin with 2 or 3 is Release 1. This is the earliest 1-2-3 and is the grandparent of all other releases and versions. It is two-dimensional, and similar in many aspects to the 2.x releases.

The other release of 1-2-3 that does not have a release number is 1-2-3 for Home. This is an economical version of Release 2.3. It is two-dimensional and has 512 rows (instead of the 8192 rows in Release 2.3). 1-2-3 for Home also has 30 Smartsheets, which are ready-to-use templates. They include calendars, accounting sheets, and other prepared forms the average user and homeowner would find useful. It has no add-ins except Wysiwyg.

Do They All Talk to Each Other?

It is important to know that files created in 1-2-3 for Home can be retrieved into the standard 2.x releases of 1-2-3. Also, files created in the standard 2.x releases can be retrieved into 1-2-3 for Home. If the file retrieved into 1-2-3 for Home has data in cells beyond the smaller limits of the 1-2-3 for Home area, however, that data will be lost.

Files created in the 2.x releases have the .WK1 extension. Files created in release 3.x have the .WK3 extension. Note that WK1 files can be retrieved into 3.x, but WK3 files cannot be retrieved into 2.x.

Force the Issue

There is a way around the refusal of 2.x to retrieve 3.x files. When you're working in 3.x, you can tell the product to save the work as a WK1 file so that it can be retrieved in 2.x. As you type the name of the file to be saved, type the .WK1 extension. It is possible to make 3.x always save files as WK1 files. The command in 3.x is /Worksheet Global Default Ext Save. Change WK3 to WK1. Now when you save, the file will have the WK1 extension and can be retrieved into the 2.x releases. One word of caution: If you save a worksheet as a WK1 file, make sure it has only one sheet. Three-dimensional (multisheet) files can't be saved as WK1 files.

Of Releases and Their Properties

The following sections provide the important properties and additions for the 2.x and 3.x DOS releases.

Release 2.01

Release 2.01 added some new functions and commands to Release 1A. It is one of the earlier versions. (2.01 and 1A are releases that were produced almost immediately after Releases 2.0 and 1.0.)

Release 2.2

The major change in Release 2.2 was the addition of ALLWAYS, which enables you to improve the appearance of a worksheet with such graphic enhancements as changed fonts, lines, shading, and colors. Other added features were Undo, macro recording, range search and replace, and the capability to refer to ranges not on the active sheet (file linking).

Release 2.3

In Release 2.3, ALLWAYS was replaced with the Wysiwyg add-in. With Wysiwyg, you can perform standard worksheet operations and add graphic enhancements without switching between display modes. Other add-ins in this release were Viewer, and Auditor.

About Release 2.3 Add-Ins

Viewer enables you to see the contents of other 1-2-3 files, and then link cells in those files to the current worksheet or retrieve the entire file. Macro Library Manager enables you to create macros that can be saved in libraries for use in other worksheets. Auditor is used to check and trace formulas.

Added @ functions, more graph types, range preselection, use of the Delete key to delete the contents of a cell, dialog boxes, background printing, and mouse support were also added.

Release 2.4

Release 2.4 had two additional add-ins, Backsolver and SmartIcons. Backsolver makes it possible to do a "what-if" from the formula to the data. In other words, you write a formula and tell Backsolver what value you want to get with the formula. Backsolver then shows you the value for

> **Icon Do It!**
>
> SmartIcons are little pictures of the most common actions you perform in 1-2-3. These are arranged in a column next to the worksheet area.

each piece of data to accomplish this goal. Release 2.4 also introduced the capability to do landscape (sideways) printing on dot-matrix printers.

Release 3.0

Release 3.0, the first three-dimensional release, included commands and keystrokes necessary to support the additional sheets. The 3-D feature enables the user to have more than one file open at a time. Undo, search and replace, and macro recording were also included in this release.

Release 3.1

Release 3.1 added a few major changes to Release 3.0. The two most important were the addition of Wysiwyg and mouse support. Release 3.1+ was released soon after 3.1 and offered the Solver, Backsolver, Viewer, and Auditor add-ins.

> **Solving the Problem**
>
> Solver is an analysis tool that offers several possible answers to a problem based on your data. It helps in making business decisions in which several factors are taken into consideration and several outcomes are possible.

Release 3.4

Release 3.4, the latest 3.x release, combined all the features discussed in other releases. For instance, it has three-dimensional capability, Wysiwyg, SmartIcons, Auditor, Viewer, file-linking capabilities, Solver, more graph styles, and added @functions. It is also considerably faster than earlier 3.x releases.

A Last Word on Your Choices

This book was written primarily for 1-2-3 for DOS, Releases 2.3 and 2.4, but offers some tips applicable to Release 3.x as well as earlier DOS releases. Although some of the information is applicable also to 1-2-3 for Windows, this is primarily a book for DOS users.

Error Messages— What They Mean and What To Do

From time to time, the serene orderly work you're doing in 1-2-3 will be interrupted by a rude beep and a box containing an error message in the middle of the screen.

Sometimes you know what you did; other times it's a complete surprise. This chapter lists some of the more common error messages and tells you how to deal with them.

Don't Rub It In

When you make a mistake, the indicator in the upper right corner of the screen flashes the word ERROR. The error box in the middle of the screen and the flashing ERROR remain until you do something about the error.

If you know what you did and don't need 1-2-3 to remind you that you made a mistake, press Esc and the error is just an ugly memory.

If you don't know what you did wrong, what do you do to correct it? The quickest way to find out what you did wrong (and find out how to correct it) is to press F1 (Help) and read the help screen about the particular problem. But that may not be enough help.

This chapter is a good resource for two reasons. It amplifies the help screens, and it can help you avoid errors. Reading this chapter can help you play the game by the rules.

Common 1-2-3 Error Messages

Here are some common error messages, listed in alphabetical order, that you're bound to run across as you use 1-2-3.

`Background print not installed`

You tried to use /**Print Background** or :**Print Background** without first typing Bprint at the DOS prompt before you started 1-2-3. If you want to use background print, you must exit from 1-2-3, type Bprint in the program directory, and restart 1-2-3.

`Cannot enable Undo; memory required is already in use`

Undo needs a lot of RAM. Your best bet if you want to enable Undo is to save, and then erase the current worksheet by choosing /**Worksheet Erase Yes**. If you still can't enable Undo, try the steps provided in Chapter 4 in the section, "What To Do If You Run Out of Memory."

Cannot initialize port

You need to be sure that the correct printer port or logical port is chosen before the printer will print. Choose /Worksheet **G**lobal **D**efault **P**rinter **I**nterface or **:P**rint **C**onfig **I**nterface to select the correct printer port.

Cannot invoke DOS

See Insufficient memory to invoke DOS.

You tried to use the /**S**ystem command to suspend 1-2-3 so that you could use DOS commands. Either reduce memory usage (see Chapter 4) or quit 1-2-3, use the DOS commands, and restart 1-2-3. If you have to exit 1-2-3, be sure to save your work first.

Cannot move or copy beyond worksheet boundaries

You tried to move or copy a group of cells to a location too close to the edge of the worksheet. You can't copy four rows to the bottom row (row 8192), there is no place for the extra three rows to go. Copy or move to cells further from the edge.

Column hidden

You tried to go to a cell that is in a hidden column, or you tried to use certain commands on cells in a hidden column. Choose /Worksheet **C**olumn **D**isplay to display the hidden columns before moving to the cell or using the command.

Directory does not exist

You configured 1-2-3 to save to or retrieve from a nonexistent directory. At the DOS prompt, create the directory, then reenter 1-2-3. An alternative is to have 1-2-3 use another directory by choosing /**F**ile **D**irectory for a temporary change, or /**W**orksheet **G**lobal **D**efault **D**irectory for a permanent change.

You also might have deleted a directory that you configured 1-2-3 to use for saving and retrieving.

It may be a network directory that is not currently available.

Disk drive not ready

You tried to save to or retrieve from a floppy disk drive that has an open door or no disk. Insert a formatted disk and close the door to the disk drive.

Disk error

You tried to copy to a disk, retrieve from a disk, or list files from a disk, but the disk has something wrong with it. It may be unformatted, damaged, or incompatible with your computer. Inspect the disk to be sure that it's not damaged. Make sure that the disk is formatted. To do that, exit from 1-2-3 and type DIR at the DOS prompt. Such error messages as Invalid media, Non-DOS disk, or Drive not ready mean that the disk is unreadable and probably not formatted. Use another disk for saving, or format the disk and then save files to it.

Disk full

You tried to save a file to a disk that is full. Erase some files or use a new disk.

Disk is write protected

You tried to save a file to a disk that has been changed so it cannot accept files. To change write protection, remove the tape covering the notch on a 5 1/4-inch floppy disk, or slide the plastic tab so the hole is open on a 3 1/2-inch floppy disk.

File does not exist

You tried to retrieve a file that does not exist or whose name you typed incorrectly. Choose /File Retrieve, and press F3 (Names) to see all the files in the current directory. Highlight the one you want to retrieve and press Enter.

File pathname too long

You cannot type more than 64 characters in the path name for a file. Choose /File Directory to make the long path name the current directory, and then retrieve the file. An alternative is to use DOS to copy the file to a directory that does not have so many characters in its path.

Graph name does not exist

You tried to go to a named graph that does not exist. When you select **:Graph G**oto, you're prompted to choose or type the name of the graph you want to move the cell pointer to. Press to see a list of valid graph names at the prompt, highlight the graph name you want to go to, and press Enter.

Incorrect password

The file was saved with a secret password. If you don't know the password, you can't retrieve the file.

Insufficient memory to invoke DOS

You tried to use the **/System** command to suspend 1-2-3 so you could use DOS commands. Either reduce memory usage (see Chapter 4) or quit 1-2-3, enter the DOS commands, and restart 1-2-3.

Invalid cell or range address

You specified a range name that does not exist or you typed a cell address incorrectly in a command or at the GoTo prompt. Be sure the range name exists and is spelled correctly. Be sure the cell address uses a column letter, and then a row number. The letter can't be higher than IV and the number can't be larger than 8192.

Invalid character in filename

You cannot use the following characters in DOS file names:

> * . ? : \ " / [ ] ¦ < > + = ; ,

These same characters are rejected when you save a file in 1-2-3. Change the file name so that it includes letters, numbers, and permissible characters. When in doubt about a character, just avoid it.

`Invalid number or Invalid number input`

A command prompted you for number input, and you typed something other than a number or you typed a number that is not allowed. Enter a number, making sure it is within range, if necessary.

`Justify range is full or line too long`

You tried to use /**Range Justify** to turn one long line of text into a paragraph, but you did not highlight enough area in the range. Highlight more cells, either downward or to the right.

`Memory full`

Certain commands and operations may use up all available RAM. See the section on memory in Chapter 4 for things you can do to correct this problem.

`Named range not found in worksheet file`

You tried to use /**File Combine** to bring a named range from another file into the current sheet, but the named range does not exist. Retrieve the other file to find the correct range name.

`No more matching strings`

The /**Range Search** command found the last string in the range you highlighted.

`No print range specified`

You chose **Go** from the **Print** menu before highlighting a range of cells to be printed. Choose /**Print Printer Range** in the main menu, or choose **:Print Range Set** in the Wysiwyg menu.

`No printer driver loaded`

You did not choose a printer when you installed 1-2-3. Exit from 1-2-3, type Install at the DOS prompt, choose Modify the Current Driver Set, and then choose Change Selected Equipment.

`Not a valid worksheet file`

You tried to retrieve a file that was not created in 1-2-3, which is possible only after you use the translate program to convert files to 1-2-3 format. Only certain file formats can be converted to 1-2-3 format. You'll have to exit 1-2-3 and type Translate at the DOS prompt and follow the resulting menus to translate a file so it can be retrieved in 1-2-3.

`Not enough memory to attach this addin`

Most add-ins require additional memory. Reduce memory usage with the steps in the section in Chapter 4, which deals with reducing memory usage.

`Printer error`

The printer is off, offline, out of paper, not selected, or not connected properly. Make sure the printer is on, is online, has paper, and is properly connected. To select the printer for use, choose /**W**orksheet **G**lobal **D**efault **P**rinter **N**ame, or choose **:P**rint **C**onfig **P**rinter.

To select the printer for use, choose /**W**orksheet **G**lobal **D**efault **P**rinter **N**ame or choose **:P**rint **C**onfig **P**rinter.

`Protected cell`

Using /**W**orksheet **G**lobal **P**rotection **E**nable puts an invisible protective shield on every cell in the worksheet. You cannot enter, change, or delete data or rows or columns anywhere. Either turn protection off by choosing /**W**orksheet **G**lobal **P**rotection **D**isable, or unprotect just the cells on which you want to work by choosing /**R**ange **U**nprotect.

`Replacement would cause cell to become invalid`

You tried to use /**R**ange **S**earch to replace a valid cell content with an invalid one. For instance, you can't replace @SUM with @SUMMARY. Check the replace string to see what you typed incorrectly.

String not found

You tried to use /**R**ange **S**earch to look for a text string that does not exist in the range the way you typed it at the command prompt. Check the command prompt to see what you typed incorrectly.

Worksheet file revision is out of date

In an earlier version of 1-2-3, you tried to retrieve a file created in a later version. This happens when you try to retrieve a file from a 3.x release (with a .WK3 extension) into a 2.x release. The file must first be saved with a .WK1 extension in the 3.x version.

Worksheet full

You tried to insert a row or a column, but data is already in the last row or column (row 8192 or column IV). Delete an empty row or column somewhere in the middle of the area, or move the data back from the edge.

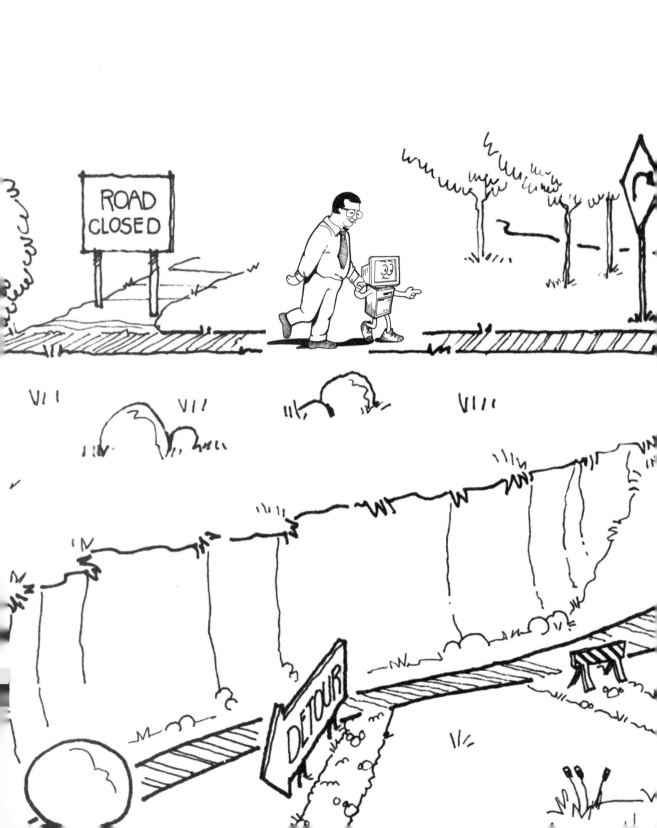

The Great 1-2-3 Troubleshooting Road Map

CHAPTER TWENTY-THREE

Here it is—the guide through all your 1-2-3 problems! Just follow us down the road until you come to the path that describes your problem. Read through the list of the most likely culprits, then turn to the chapter referenced for additional information. If you don't encounter any roadblocks, congratulations—1-2-3 is working just fine for you!

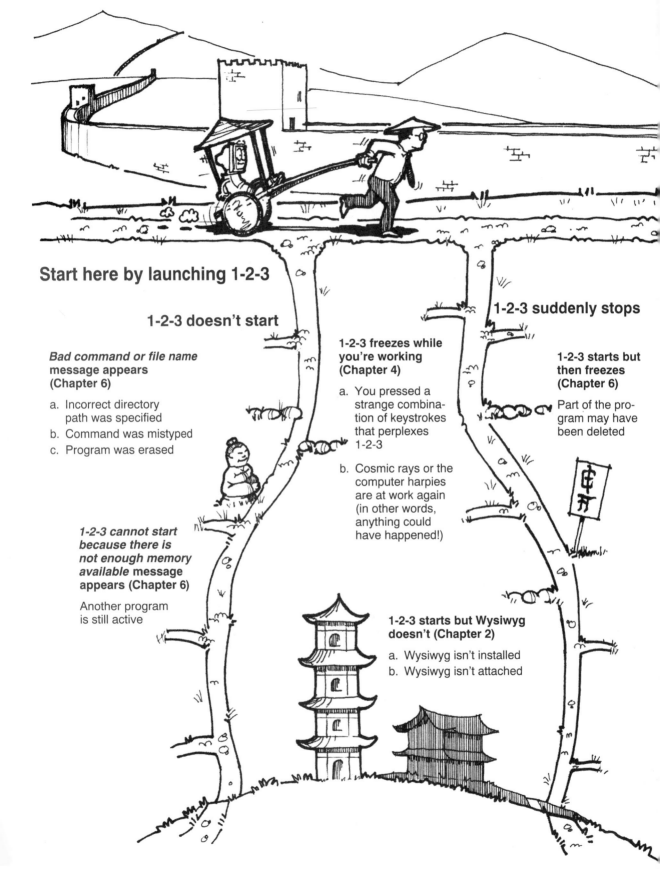

Start here by launching 1-2-3

1-2-3 doesn't start

Bad command or file name message appears (Chapter 6)

a. Incorrect directory path was specified
b. Command was mistyped
c. Program was erased

1-2-3 cannot start because there is not enough memory available message appears (Chapter 6)

Another program is still active

1-2-3 freezes while you're working (Chapter 4)

a. You pressed a strange combination of keystrokes that perplexes 1-2-3

b. Cosmic rays or the computer harpies are at work again (in other words, anything could have happened!)

1-2-3 suddenly stops

1-2-3 starts but then freezes (Chapter 6)

Part of the program may have been deleted

1-2-3 starts but Wysiwyg doesn't (Chapter 2)

a. Wysiwyg isn't installed
b. Wysiwyg isn't attached

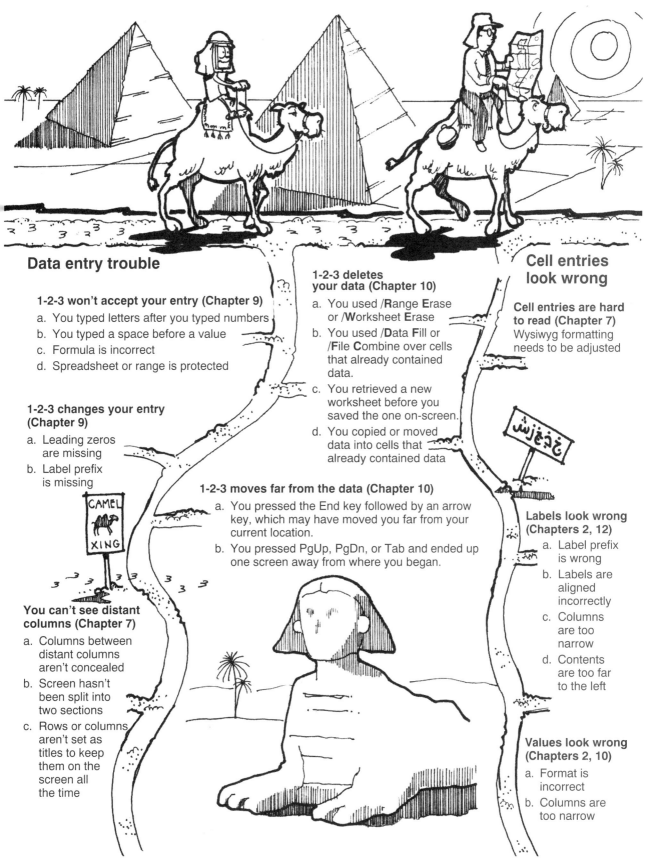

Data entry trouble

1-2-3 won't accept your entry (Chapter 9)

a. You typed letters after you typed numbers

b. You typed a space before a value

c. Formula is incorrect

d. Spreadsheet or range is protected

1-2-3 changes your entry (Chapter 9)

a. Leading zeros are missing

b. Label prefix is missing

You can't see distant columns (Chapter 7)

a. Columns between distant columns aren't concealed

b. Screen hasn't been split into two sections

c. Rows or columns aren't set as titles to keep them on the screen all the time

1-2-3 deletes your data (Chapter 10)

a. You used /Range Erase or /Worksheet Erase

b. You used /Data Fill or /File Combine over cells that already contained data.

c. You retrieved a new worksheet before you saved the one on-screen.

d. You copied or moved data into cells that already contained data

1-2-3 moves far from the data (Chapter 10)

a. You pressed the End key followed by an arrow key, which may have moved you far from your current location.

b. You pressed PgUp, PgDn, or Tab and ended up one screen away from where you began.

Cell entries look wrong

Cell entries are hard to read (Chapter 7)
Wysiwyg formatting needs to be adjusted

Labels look wrong (Chapters 2, 12)

a. Label prefix is wrong

b. Labels are aligned incorrectly

c. Columns are too narrow

d. Contents are too far to the left

Values look wrong (Chapters 2, 10)

a. Format is incorrect

b. Columns are too narrow

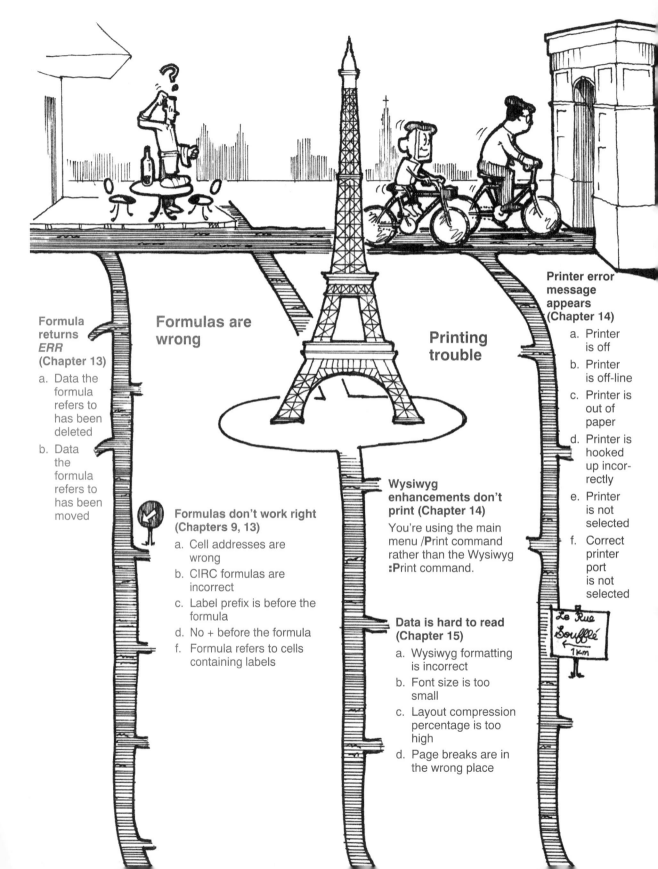

Formula returns *ERR* (Chapter 13)

a. Data the formula refers to has been deleted

b. Data the formula refers to has been moved

Formulas are wrong

Formulas don't work right (Chapters 9, 13)

a. Cell addresses are wrong

b. CIRC formulas are incorrect

c. Label prefix is before the formula

d. No + before the formula

f. Formula refers to cells containing labels

Printing trouble

Wysiwyg enhancements don't print (Chapter 14)

You're using the main menu /**P**rint command rather than the Wysiwyg :**P**rint command.

Data is hard to read (Chapter 15)

a. Wysiwyg formatting is incorrect

b. Font size is too small

c. Layout compression percentage is too high

d. Page breaks are in the wrong place

Printer error message appears (Chapter 14)

a. Printer is off

b. Printer is off-line

c. Printer is out of paper

d. Printer is hooked up incorrectly

e. Printer is not selected

f. Correct printer port is not selected

Le Rue Soufflé
← 1 km

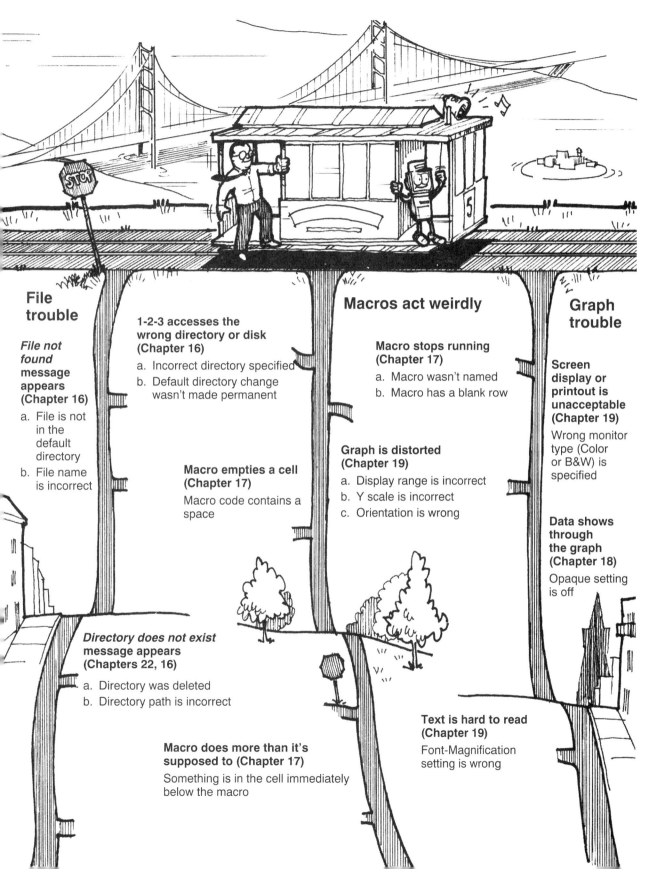

File trouble

File not found message appears (Chapter 16)

a. File is not in the default directory
b. File name is incorrect

1-2-3 accesses the wrong directory or disk (Chapter 16)

a. Incorrect directory specified
b. Default directory change wasn't made permanent

Macro empties a cell (Chapter 17)

Macro code contains a space

Directory does not exist message appears (Chapters 22, 16)

a. Directory was deleted
b. Directory path is incorrect

Macro does more than it's supposed to (Chapter 17)

Something is in the cell immediately below the macro

Macros act weirdly

Macro stops running (Chapter 17)

a. Macro wasn't named
b. Macro has a blank row

Graph is distorted (Chapter 19)

a. Display range is incorrect
b. Y scale is incorrect
c. Orientation is wrong

Text is hard to read (Chapter 19)

Font-Magnification setting is wrong

Graph trouble

Screen display or printout is unacceptable (Chapter 19)

Wrong monitor type (Color or B&W) is specified

Data shows through the graph (Chapter 18)

Opaque setting is off

The Oops! 1-2-3 Glossary

@ functions   Formulas that begin with the @ (at) symbol and that expand the variety of formulas available to the user.

absolute cell reference   A cell specified in a formula is a cell reference. It becomes an absolute cell reference when dollar signs are used in front of the column letter and row number. That specific cell will always be used in the formula, regardless of where the formula is copied.

active area   The range containing the worksheet's data.

add-in   Extra parts of the 1-2-3 program that can be attached for use, and detached if not needed. They include Auditor, Solver, Backsolver, SmartIcons, Wysiwyg, Macro Library Manager, and Viewer.

alignment   The placement of a label in the cell—left, right, or center.

anchor   To pin the cell pointer in a cell so that it can be expanded to highlight several other cells.

Auditor   An add-in that allows the user to diagnose the formulas in a worksheet and verify the accuracy of figures.

Backsolver   An add-in that can solve problems in reverse. A user can specify desired results and the add-in then suggests values for referenced data that will obtain the desired results.

backup   Copies of files stored separately from the original file. Creating a backup guarantees that if the original file is lost or corrupted, a copy will still be available.

boot   To start the computer.

border cells   Cells at the edge of the worksheet area, in columns A and IV and rows 1 and 8192.

borders   Specified rows and/or columns to be printed on every page to make a large worksheet easier to read.

cell   The intersection of a row and a column. The unit of a worksheet where labels, values, or formulas are entered.

cell address   The column letter and row number that identifies a specific cell.

cell entry   The contents of a cell.

cell pointer   The rectangular highlight that indicates the location of the current cell. Only one cell at a time can contain the cell pointer, which makes that cell the active cell into which data can be entered.

cell reference   The cell named in a formula.

circular formula   A formula that refers to its own cell. As data entry proceeds, the formula's answer becomes increasingly inaccurate.

command   An action chosen from a menu to be performed in 1-2-3.

compression   The shrinking or stretching of a print range so it will fit on a piece of paper.

control panel   The top three lines of the display screen, above the worksheet frame.

copy   To create duplicates of a cell or a range of cells and place them elsewhere in the worksheet.

crash   When the computer or the program stops working.

criteria   In data commands, the identification of specific qualities data must have to be processed or included in calculations.

database   An organized collection of information arranged into rows and columns.

default   Settings or procedures that happen automatically on a computer or in a program. The default (normal) column width in 1-2-3 is 9 characters.

delete   To remove the contents of a cell, or to remove an entire row or column and its contents.

dialog box   A screen that appears when certain commands are chosen, which allows the user to change settings on-screen.

directory   A grouping of files on a disk; each directory can contain multiple files, as well as *subdirectories*.

display mode   The way the worksheet is shown to the user. Choices are text, graphic, color, and black and white.

DOS   Disk Operating System. The program that begins when the computer starts and is used to start other programs, run the computer, and manipulate files.

edit   To change the contents of a cell or a dialog box.

erase   To remove a file from disk or to clear a worksheet from the screen.

extract   A data query command included in a query in which specified records are displayed in a separate range. Also a file command that saves part of a worksheet to a separate file.

fields   The individual types of data in a database. First name, last name, and phone number can be field names in a database.

file   A piece of a program or the data created by a user in that program, which is stored on disk with a specific identifying name.

find   A data query command that locates certain records in a database and highlights them.

font   A collection of letters and numbers that have a unique type style and type size.

footer   Text that appears at the bottom of every printed page.

format   The way text and numbers are displayed.

formula   A cell entry that defines the relationship between two or more values.

frame   The upside down *L* at the left and top of the worksheet that contains the row numbers and column letters.

freezing   When a program or a computer stops working.

function keys   The 10 or 12 keys labeled F1, F2, and so on, which are assigned specific jobs in particular pieces of software.

global   A group of commands that affects the entire worksheet.

graph   A picture created from worksheet data to make the data easier to interpret.

graphic   Any picture added to a worksheet.

grid   Dotted horizontal and vertical lines placed around all cells in a worksheet, or the horizontal and/or vertical lines placed in a graph.

hardware cursor   The little dash that appears in the cell pointer.

header   Text that appears at the top of every printed page.

highlight   Specifying a cell or a group of cells by placing the cell pointer at that location.

icon   A small picture of a command that can be used to make the command execute.

indicator   The box in the upper right corner of the screen that shows the status of the 1-2-3 program or the cell entry.

install   A separate program used to configure and place software on a hard disk. The program is also used to change certain hardware and software settings.

label   A cell entry that begins with a *label prefix* and has a numerical value of zero.

label prefix   A mark that turns any cell entry into a label and determines its alignment in the cell. There are four: the apostrophe (')

left-aligns a label, the quotation mark (") right-aligns it, the caret (^) centers it, and the backslash (\) causes the cell entry to be repeated until it fills the cell.

landscape   Printing sideways. The long side of the paper is across the top.

link   To call data from a cell or range in another file into the current sheet.

macro   Recorded keystrokes that can be played back at another time to speed up tasks, to automate repetitive tasks, or to streamline complicated tasks.

Macro Library Manager   An add-in that allows the user to save macros in libraries for use in any worksheet.

memory   Temporary storage for data and instructions. Memory is active when the computer is on, it's emptied when the computer is turned off, and it's partially emptied when the user exits from a program. See *RAM*.

menu   A list of operations the user can perform in 1-2-3. There are two menus in 1-2-3: the main menu invoked with the slash (/) and the Wysiwyg menu invoked with the colon (:).

mouse   A device plugged into the computer that rolls around a flat surface, controls a small indicator on-screen, and allows the user to perform certain operations more quickly by clicking its button.

move   To cause cell or range contents to disappear from their current location and appear in a new cell or range.

named styles   In Wysiwyg, applying a name to the Wysiwyg enhancements to a cell so that they all can be applied at once to another cell or range.

off-sheet reference   A cell that refers to a cell in another file. See also *link*.

page break   Row or column specified by the user as a place where a new printed page should begin.

password   A secret series of keystrokes added to a file name to make it impossible for anyone who doesn't know the password to retrieve the file from disk.

portrait   Printing a document with the short side of the paper across the top.

preview   A view of a print range on-screen that shows how it will look when it's printed.

primary key   In sorting a database, the column of data that determines the order of the data after sorting.

printgraph   A separate program used to print graphs saved as .PIC files. In earlier releases of 1-2-3, it was necessary to use this program to print graphs. With current releases, the graph can be placed in the worksheet and printed with the Wysiwyg print command.

prompt   A request from the software for some kind of input from the user.

protection   A command that makes it impossible to enter data in cells.

query   A command that searches a database for particular records.

RAM   Random-Access Memory. Often called memory. See *memory*.

range   A rectangular group of cells.

range names   Names applied to ranges that make navigation, formula writing, and commands easier.

records   Rows of data in databases. Each record is the data for a separate entry in the database.

relative cell reference   A cell reference in a formula that changes to different cells when the formula is copied to other cells.

release   A copy of a product that differs from other copies because of the presence or lack of certain additional features.

retrieve   To get a file from disk and display it on-screen so that it can be viewed and changed.

scale   A difference between the highest and lowest value on the x- and y-axes of a graph.

secondary key   The column of data that *breaks ties* when data is sorted. If the primary key has two identical entries, the secondary key determines which will appear first after sorting.

shade   Darkening of cells or ranges.

Solver   An add-in that allows the user to set data to certain values and see several possible outcomes. Used often in business projections and analyses.

sort   To rearrange a database in numerical or alphabetical order.

subdirectory   A subsidiary directory located off a main directory.

tick   The individual marks on a graph's X- and Y-scales.

titles   Rows or columns designated to stay on-screen, regardless of where the cell pointer moves.

transpose   To reverse the display of a range. Rows become columns, and columns become rows.

TSR   Terminate-and-stay-resident. Certain

programs external to 1-2-3 that remain in the background (in the computer's memory) while 1-2-3 is active.

unprotect   To remove protection from a cell or range so data can be changed or deleted in those cells.

value   A cell entry that has numerical value. It may be a formula or series of digits. It must not include letters or spaces and it must not have a label prefix.

version   A copy of 1-2-3 used on a specific type of computer or in a specific operating environment.

Viewer   An add-in that allows the user to see other files while working on one file. Viewer can be used to retrieve a new file, link cells or ranges into the current sheet, or browse through other files.

Windows   An operating system that works *on top* of DOS and provides a graphical user interface.

worksheet   An array of rows and columns displayed on a computer that allows data entry and automatic calculations.

Wysiwyg   A 1-2-3 add-in that allows graphic enhancements to both the screen display and printout; also an acronym for *What you see is what you get*.

zoom   Increasing or decreasing the size of the display on-screen.

Index

Symbols

A

Q-R

Query (F7) function key, 129
quotation mark (") label prefix,
   101

RAM (random-access memory),
   41, 196, 290
/Range Erase, 28, 39, 93, 113,
   115
/Range Format, 140, 184, 188
/Range Format command, 27
/Range Format Currency, 142
/Range Format Date, 191, 254
/Range Format Fixed, 146
/Range Format Hidden, 120
/Range Format Percent 2, 190
/Range Format Reset, 145-146,
   189
/Range Input, 58
/Range Justify, 144
/Range Label, 186
/Range Label Center, 78
/Range Label Left, 78
/Range Label Right, 78
/Range Name Create, 92, 156,
   211
/Range Name Table, 256
range names, 40
   deleting, 40
   formulas, 156
   macros, 40, 218
   moving cells, 40
   symbols, 40
range preselection, 185
/Range Search, 147
/Range Transpose, 147
/Range Unprotect, 41, 58, 103
/Range Value, 161, 253

ranges, 290
   assignments, 40
   clearing, 39
   copying, 88, 95-96
      records to, 127
   erasing, 115
   extracting, 51
   filling, 112
   formatting, 27-28, 140, 142,
      189
   highlighting, 140, 142-148
      removing, 143
      sticky with Print com-
         mand, 173-174
   labels, alignment, 143
   names, 290
   printing, 173
   separate files, 51
   sticky commands, 143
   unprotected, 50
   see also criteria range; input
      range; output range; print
      range; range names
rebooting (Ctrl+Alt+Del), 46
records (databases), 126, 290
   copying to output range, 127
   deleting, 127
   extracting, 127, 129
      to output range, 132
   finding, 129
recovery, 115
rectangles, 237
redisplaying hidden columns, 59
reducing
   active area (worksheets),
      50-51

print range, 174
size, worksheets, 51
referencing cells
absolute, 285
relative, 290
reformatting
cells, 190
numbers (asterisk display),
121
reinstalling 1-2-3, 70
relative cell references, 152, 290
adjusting after copy, 93
copying formulas, 89
release numbers (versions), 20
removing highlighting, 143
renaming files, 37
:Replace, 80
replacing files, 198, 205
Reset option, 120
resetting
formats, 145
Hidden format, 146
RESTORE (DOS) command, 61
restoring directories, 59
restricting input, 58
results (formulas)
combined files, 159-160
labels, 192
no change after edit, 153
@SUM, 156
zeros, 155
retrieving files, 48, 290
automatically, 203
can't find, 201
from another version, 202
from floppy disk, 61

from specific directory, 59
worksheet disappears, 203
reversing columns/rows, 147
rounding, 146
rows
deleting
data, 115-116
zero formula results, 155
height, 80
reversing with columns, 147
titles, 76
printing, 177
running macros, 212-213

S

saving, 57
extracted worksheets, 206
files, 31, 196
backups, 37, 198
existing name, 205
first time, 198
incorrect directory, 200
over files, 205
passwords, 41, 205
path name, 201
replacing, 198, 205
to specific directory, 59
frequency, 197
graphs, 236
settings, 84
worksheets as text file, 166
scaling graphs, 242, 290
screen, 251
clearing worksheets, 113
color, 74
splitting, 42, 77
see also display

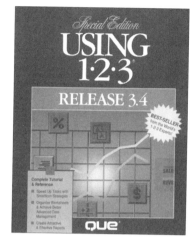

Que—The Top Name in Spreadsheet Information!

Using 1-2-3 Release 2.4,
Special Edition

Que Development Group

This performance-boosting tutorial/
reference for the latest version of
1-2-3 DOS provides tips and advice
on how to improve worksheet,
database, and graphics performance.
Includes special icons to highlight
the new features of this latest
version.

Through Version 2.4

$29.95 USA
0-88022-988-8, 1,000 pp., 7³/₈ x 9¹/₄

1-2-3 Release 2.4
QuickStart

Rick Winter

This quick tutorial to building
spreadsheets provides step-by-step
instructions on entering data and
producing graphs and reports. This
book explains how to plan and manage
databases, and features chapter
summaries to review major commands
and procedure.

Through Version 2.4

$21.95 USA
0-88022-986-1, 500 pp., 7³/₈ x 9¹/₄

1-2-3 Release 2.4
Quick Reference

Joyce J. Nielson

Through Version 2.4

$9.95 USA
0-88022-987-X, 160 pp., 4³/₄ x 8

Learning is Easy with Easy Books from Que!

Que's Easy Series offers a revolutionary concept in computer training. The friendly, 4-color interior, easy format, and simple explanations guarantee success for even the most intimidated computer user!

Easy WordPerfect
Version 5.1
$19.95 USA
0-88022-797-4, 200 pp., 8 x 10

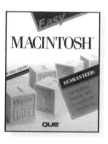

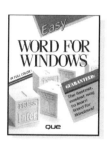

Complete Computer Coverage

Que's 1993 Computer Buyer's Guide

Que Development Group

This absolute must-have guide
packed with comparisons, recommendations,
and tips for asking all the right questions
familiarizes the reader with terms they
will need to know. This book offers a
complete analysis of both hardware and
software products, and it's loaded
with charts and tables
of product comparisons.

IBM-compatibles, Apple, & Macintosh
$14.95 USA

1-56529-021-6, 450 pp., 8 x 10

Que's Computer User's Dictionary, 3rd Edition

Bryan Pfaffenberger

This compact, practical reference contains
hundreds of definitions, explanations, examples,
and illustrations on topics from programming
to desktop publishing. You can master the
"language" of computers and learn how to make
your personal computer more efficient and more
powerful. Filled with tips and cautions, *Que's
Computer User's Dictionary* is the perfect
resource for anyone who uses a computer.

*IBM, Macintosh, Apple,
& Programming*

$12.95 USA

1-56529-023-2, 600 pp., 4³/₄ x 8

To Order, Call:
(800) 428-5331 OR (317) 573-2500